Reputable Conduct

D1401242

Date Due			

Reputable Conduct
Ethical Issues in Policing and Corrections

John R. Jones, M.Ed., Ph.D.
Law and Justice Centre,
Sir Sandford Fleming College

Prentice Hall Canada Career & Technology
Scarborough, Ontario

Canadian Cataloguing in Publication Data

Jones, John Raymond, 1943-
  Reputable conduct

ISBN 0-13-958000-X

1. Police ethics.   2. Corrections – Moral and ethical aspects.
I. Title

HV7924.J66 1998   174'.93632   C97-931732-0

 © 1998 Prentice-Hall Canada Inc., Scarborough, Ontario
A Division of Simon & Schuster/A Viacom Company

Prentice-Hall, Inc., Upper Saddle River, New Jersey
Prentice-Hall International (UK) Limited, London
Prentice-Hall of Australia, Pty. Limited, Sydney
Prentice-Hall Hispanoamericana, S.A., Mexico City
Prentice-Hall of India Private Limited, New Delhi
Prentice-Hall of Japan, Inc., Tokyo
Simon & Schuster Southeast Asia Private Limited, Singapore
Editora Prentice-Hall do Brasil, Ltda., Rio de Janeiro

ISBN 0-13-958000-X

Vice President, Editorial Director: Laura Pearson
Acquisitions Editor: David Stover
Executive Marketing Manager: Jo-Ann DeLuca
Production Editor: Andrew Winton
Copy Editor: Allyson Latta
Production Coordinator: Leora Conway
Permissions: Susan Wallace-Cox
Cover and Interior Design: Monica Kompter
Cover Image: PhotoDisc
Page Layout: Arlene Edgar

  2 3 4 5   RRD   02 01 00 99 98

Printed and bound in United States of America.

Visit the Prentice Hall Canada web site! Send us your comments,
browse our catalogues, and more at **www.phcanada.com**.
Or reach us through e-mail at **phabinfo_pubcanada@prenhall.com**.

To my wife Marilyn, and my three children, Steffan, Christopher, and Melissa, who have brought more love and meaning to my life than words can express. This book is also dedicated to the memory of my mother, Elizabeth Jones, whose generosity of spirit has left an indelible mark on my life.

Table of Contents

Chapter 9   Reputable Officers   **135**

Preface

Written for students in college justice programs, and for police and correctional officers in training, *Reputable Conduct* has been designed to be used as a working text rather than a reference book. The book has its roots in my own experience of teaching ethics for the last 17 years, and I thank my students for the great deal they have taught me during that time. My experience has influenced the very personal tone of the writing style used in the book. As I wrote it, I imagined my students listening to me.

Reputable Conduct is intended to be a friendly and easy-to-read introduction to the difficult and sometimes peculiar ethical demands of the professions of policing and corrections. It addresses some of the characteristics of these roles, with particular emphasis on subcultural constraints, and how loyalty to our colleague group can sometimes cause us to sacrifice our individuality. How these constraints may affect the moral decision-making of an officer is looked at in detail in chapters 4, 5 and 6.

One unusual feature of the book is the discussion in Chapter 3, which encourages the student to think about the role of the ethics educator. The discussion has been included so that the educator's role can be more clearly understood by the student. I hope this will reduce the possibility of misunderstanding arising between teacher and student regarding the purpose of an ethics course.

Tools that may be helpful for resolving moral dilemmas are discussed in Chapter 7. Chapter 8 includes several case studies to give students an opportunity to practise using these tools.

Some of the material in the book could be described as sensitive—even controversial—in nature. To gain maximum benefit from the experience of working through the book, students are encouraged to consider with an open mind the readings and the Reflections, which are searching questions interspersed throughout each chapter and based on the preceding content. This will require a degree of maturity and discipline.

Reputable Conduct is designed to provide students with a vehicle to promote private thought and class discussion about issues that—from what I have been told by my students and many practitioners over the years—are important to the vital roles played in our society by police and correctional officers.

If such thinking and discussion contributes, even in some small way, to justice continuing to be served, and to the individual officer's sense of well-being being enhanced, then the effort on all our parts will have been justified.

Acknowledgments

It has been a pleasure to work with staff members of Prentice Hall Canada Career & Technology in the writing of this book, my first attempt at such an enterprise. They have been unfailingly helpful, cooperative and encouraging.

I wish to acknowledge the early and continuing work of David Stover, Acquisitions Editor. David has been a gracious contract negotiator and guide. His early suggestions for improving the book were invaluable. Ivetka Vasil, Editorial Assistant, undertook the review process and kept me informed in a most supportive way. Andrew Winton, Production Editor, shepherded the book through the production phase and did so with class and a little firmness when it was required. And I wish to acknowledge the expert help and advice of Allyson Latta, whose copyediting contributed greatly to improving the original manuscript.

Finally, I wish to say how much I valued the feedback received from the external reviewers: Janet Hoffman, Lambton College; Lori Larsen, Lethbridge Community College; Ann Parks, Lethbridge Community College; Rebecca Volk, Algonquin College; Megan Way Nicholson, St. Lawrence College; and Lisa Bezaire, Sir Sandford Fleming College. Their encouraging and constructive comments gave me the will to finish the book, and much food for thought. Some of their suggestions have been incorporated in this edition, and others have been kept on file for inclusion in what, I hope, will be subsequent editions of this book.

J.R.J.

About the Author

Dr. John Jones has worked for more than 30 years in the human development field, as as minister, hospital chaplain, youth leader, correctional officer, high school teacher, probation officer and correctional institution administrator. During the last 17 years he has worked as an administrator and professor in the Law and Justice Centre at a Canadian college of applied arts and technology, where he has enjoyed teaching ethics to justice students.

John has also been active in training and consulting in the justice field. He has trained several thousand participants in Ethics in the Workplace, Team Development with an Ethical Twist, and Hostage Survival Skills. He is considered to be a caring, compassionate, humorous and skilled facilitator, seminar leader and speaker.

John holds a joint Honours Bachelor of Arts degree in psychology and philosophy from the University of Wales, Cardiff; a Master of Education degree from the University of Toronto (The Ontario Institute for Studies in Education); and a Doctor of Philosophy degree from the University of Toronto.

John has lived and worked in Britain, Jamaica, Australia and Canada. He is married with three children.

Reputable Conduct

Introduction

Perhaps the most important thing I learned from this class is that from now on I should always do the following:

- Keep an open mind about every issue
- Try to look at an issue from as many perspectives as possible, before I form an opinion
- Test my bias on issues about which I've formed an opinion
- Realize that because everyone doesn't look at life's issues in the same way that I do, doesn't make them wrong and me right
- I should not be ashamed to change my opinion on an issue when I had earlier felt the opposite
- This class helped to make me aware of how grey many of life's issues are—there are few issues that are really black or white.

— Journal entry. Justice student in ethics course.

I think that an ethical person is someone who is consistent in doing the "right" thing. Being ethical consists of determining what is morally correct, and standing up for what you believe is right. I think an ethical person is a confident person. Someone who is not influenced by others from what is the morally correct action to be taken in a given situation. I see myself as an ethical person but lack the confidence to stand up for every moral issue or ethical dilemma that I encounter.

— Journal entry. Justice student in ethics course.

After reading this chapter, you should be able to

- *Explain the purpose of this book*
- *Explain how we may have arrived at our values*
- *Explain how we in the justice field may inherit values*
- *Explain the notion of **subculture** in policing and corrections*
- *Apply knowledge of subculture in the military to policing and corrections*
- *Explain the notion of **de-individuation***

Why This Book?

For the last 17 years I have taught a course in ethics to students in the Law and Justice Centre of a Canadian college of applied arts and technology. For an equal number of years I have enquired of visiting publishers' representatives regarding texts available with respect to ethics education in the criminal justice field. The answer has always been that they know of little in this area. In addition, some of my faculty colleagues in other colleges, and some police and corrections training personnel, have asked me about such texts. On several occasions I was asked a similar question during a 1996 lecture tour of Australia.

That these enquiries are being made is encouraging, for there appears to be a growing interest in ethics training in the justice field. But the enquiries, along with some direct personal requests of me to do something concrete to meet the need, have translated into a personal challenge. You are now reading my response to that challenge.

What Kind of Book Is This?

This book is not intended to be a theoretical discourse on ethics. Background historical and theoretical information on ethics can be found, for example, in virtually any medical or business ethics text. This information is fairly consistently addressed in these texts and I think it would be redundant to cover similar ground here. Rather, this book is designed to be a practical work with direct application to instructors and practitioners in the justice field, and to their students. It is written and designed to be a resource in the classroom—both to the teacher delivering an ethics course, and most importantly to you the student. My hope is that this book will become a *working* text; that it will become well-thumbed by the end of the educational experience for which it is being used.

Much of the content of this work is characterized by an approach that I can only describe as deeply personal, and for this I beg the reader's indulgence. My experience gained as a correctional worker and institution administrator before I became a college professor, serves as a foundation for much of what is discussed. And many of the ideas in the book spring from 17 years of trial and error on my part as a college professor working in a college justice department, as I have attempted to address ethical issues in my own ethics courses. It has been both a privilege and a challenge to work with students over the years, and they have taught me much. The book's genesis and content have also been influenced by the experience I have gained in conducting ethics seminars with about 2,000 participants from various justice departments in Canada and Australia. As with my students, these participants have also contributed greatly to my learning. The work also has its roots in the research I completed for a Ph.D. dissertation at the University of Toronto.

Briefly, the dissertation addressed ethics teaching in the justice field; it also examined the potential effects of officer subculture on the ability of individual officers to make independent moral decisions in their (justice) workplace. The dissertation employed a qualitative research methodology, which means that much of the data was gathered through in-depth interviews with practitioners from the justice field. Most, but not all, of these interviews were with correctional officers and administrators. Disappointingly, I experienced some difficulty obtaining cooperation from police forces for the purposes of interviewing their staff about this sensitive dissertation topic. Since completing my dissertation, however, I have had access to a number of police personnel who were prepared to be interviewed for this book.

Reputable Conduct, then, is clearly coloured by my own personal experience as a worker and administrator in corrections, by what I have learned from students and participants in my ethics courses and seminars, and from the research for my Ph.D. dissertation.

The Design of the Text

Though designed to be thought-provoking, this text is not designed to condemn or accuse or point a finger. The roles of the correctional officer and the police officer are often demanding and extraordinarily complex ones. It would be improper, therefore, for this text, or any similar text for that matter, to peddle a particular point of view with respect to the complex ethical issues that often emerge from this kind of work. There may be times when you feel, however, because of the nature of the challenges presented and the questions asked, that there is a hidden agenda; that is, that there is a preferred way of thinking about a given issue and that you are being led in that direction. Because students can sometimes feel this way, there is a discussion in Chapter 3 about what I call the lurking dangers of indoctrination, or the perception by students of indoctrination by the teacher. The intention of this book is not to lead you in any particular direction or to tell you what you should do in a given situation. The intention is to prod, push and poke you into thinking more deeply about what, it would seem to me, are important ethical issues and moral dilemmas facing those of us involved in the justice field.

If the discussions and dilemmas are on occasion posed in a manner that causes you to feel that you are being judged, this is because they are designed to be searching and challenging. It is, of course, not my intention to stand in judgment over you the reader. On many occasions, I have personally confronted similar dilemmas in my own career as a correctional officer and as an institution administrator, and only a foolish person would claim infallibility in dealing with such dilemmas. Because of my own struggles, and the struggles of others who have conveyed their stories to me, my approach, hopefully, is one characterized by compassion. But this does not mean that we should shy away from asking each other some hard questions about our work. As is the case with almost any field of ethical enquiry, there are many more questions than there are answers, so throughout the text we will be stopping, under the heading Reflections, to ask some of these questions.

Perhaps an appropriate first challenge might be for you to debate whether talking about moral dilemmas facing us in our daily work is a worthwhile activity.

Reflections

Might we learn something from considering alternative perspectives of colleagues, subordinates or superiors?

Is there anyone who has a monopoly on wisdom with respect to the dilemmas we face daily?

Should we go it alone with these dilemmas; that is, work out our own solutions in isolation from our colleagues?

Should we find out what our peers think about specific issues and follow the consensus?

Where does talking about moral dilemmas and their resolution rate as a teaching priority? What about moral, as well as legal, personal accountability?

Does moral accountability matter enough to us to warrant serious discussion about serious issues?

Can this difficult job we do cause our sense of what is right or wrong to become jaded?

Can our moral sense be changed, or sensitized or perhaps reawakened?

These are, in my view, examples of important questions deserving serious attention. Perhaps you will consider this point of view itself worthy of discussion. If you disagree with me, then you should be able to give reasons for your disagreement. In any event, the above examples are the sort of questions that will be asked from time to time throughout the book. It would be an interesting exercise for you—at the *end* of the book and your course—to reflect on whether you would make any changes in the way you earlier attempted to answer the questions.

Is There a Link Between Ethics Education and Moral Behaviour?

The text aspires to be grist for the discussion mill because I believe that conversation about moral dilemmas and their resolutions has the potential to heighten awareness of personal moral responsibility. Derek Bok (1988), while president of Harvard University, wrote a thought-provoking article called "Can Higher Education Foster Higher Morals?" Bok says:

> Skeptics will reply that courses in moral reasoning have no effect on behaviour, but this criticism seems overdrawn. To be sure, no instruction can suffice to turn a scoundrel into a virtuous human being. But most young people arrive at the university with decent instincts and a genuine concern for others. For them, courses that foster an ability to detect ethical issues more perceptively, to think about them more carefully, to understand more clearly the reasons for acting morally seem likely not only to train their minds but to have a positive effect on their behaviour as well. (p. 7)

Of course, Bok's notion that most young people arrive at university with decent instincts and a genuine concern for others would apply not only to those of you at university, but equally to those of you in college justice departments, and in police and corrections training facilities.

I tend to agree with Bok. We have to be realistic about the possible effects of ethics courses, but the potential is there, I believe, for informed and critical reflection and thought to translate into a greater desire to do what one considers to be the right thing. But what I think about this issue is not the important thing. What matters most is what you think.

Reflections

What do you think of Bok's point of view?

Do you believe that thinking more clearly about ethical issues and moral dilemmas has any potential for helping you do what you consider to be the right thing?

The Place of Courage in Ethics Education

Taking time out in a course like this to think about ethical issues may also have the potential to foster moral courage; that is, having worked out what we should do in a given situation, we may have the fortitude to do it, irrespective of the forces pulling us in other directions.

But the first sign of courage, perhaps, is for each of us to be willing to face up to the hard questions posed earlier, and others like them in this text. To risk the intellectual, psychological and emotional discomfort that will invariably result from such honest enquiry is a bold step. It can be disturbing to find that the result of such enquiry is simply, on occasion, little more than the replacing of answers we thought we had with troubling questions concerning those "answers." It can be equally disturbing to be confronted with the thought that if we are to be honest with ourselves, our particular way of looking at something, or a particular value we have held for some time, may need revision—if not complete re-thinking.

Students often talk about being somewhat scared of confronting their biases and prejudices. The good news is that those who show the willingness and the courage to submit their values and ideas to scrutiny, often feel they are stronger for the experience. One of my students, referring to his personal growth, wrote at the end of an ethics course: "Not only does this course challenge your existing values and norms, I found myself asking why do I think like this? and what causes me to think like this?...I think if you are comfortable with this self-examination, that it opens up doors for self-growth." Another wrote: "We were afraid and we grew....I have realized that being afraid is normal." And another: "This has been a challenging class. While I have often left the room with a headache it has certainly made up for it in other ways. True morals are those that can be challenged openly and objectively. If a person can do that and still believe in that moral, then it is certainly a moral that should be believed in."

Reflections

Is being willing to submit your views and values to a significant challenge the kind of activity you consider requires courage?

Or, is it a foolhardy exercise, at best likely only to reduce our general happiness, at worst likely to confuse us totally?

There are people who would argue, and possibly with some justification, that unless we are able and willing to test our views and our values by the fire of honest enquiry and soul-searching, that a) the values are not truly our own, and therefore, b) they are not worth having. Many of our views and values, it is argued, are inherited; put on, as it were, as we would a suit of clothes. We have just assumed them, often without paying much attention or thought to how we arrived at them. If this is the case, then perhaps we should call them habits rather than values. What do you think?

Inheriting "Values" in the Justice Field

Some would argue that the tendency toward inheriting views and values described in the Reflections segment above applies *particularly* to those of us who work in the justice field. Some would take it a step further and argue that to resist inheriting or adopting the values of our colleague group is a decision fraught with some risk. These values are what we sometimes call norms. For example, Frederick Desroches (1986), a sociology professor at a Canadian university, speaking of new recruits to police work, makes the point:

> From association with fellow police officers, and by being sensitive to their attitudes and beliefs, the new recruit soon picks up on the general group's opinion about most police matters....Once a subculture has been formed, novices entering the group are confronted with a 'fait accompli'—a set of norms and values to which they are exposed and are expected to conform. (p. 40)

And Grossi and Berg (1991), in the corrections context, make a similar point:

Again, it may be that in order to attain a satisfactory level of peer support, and reduce conflicting pressures endemic to correctional institutions, correctional officers must compromise their personal values and interests. (p. 80)

Clearly, these are sobering and troubling sentiments. The writers indicate that to survive as a police or correctional officer in terms of early and continuing acceptance by peers, an individual officer would have difficulty operating as an independent person, doing his own thinking about moral dilemmas encountered on the job. Desroches talks about police officers, especially new ones, having to conform to group norms and values. Grossi and Berg, in talking about correctional officers, take the idea one step further and talk about the requirement to compromise personal values and interests in order to continue being accepted by peers.

Later we will discuss this issue of colleague loyalty, or peer pressure, if you like, in greater depth. The issue has to do with *subculture* in policing and corrections, and how it can impact on individual officers.

Reflections

What do you think of the views of these researchers and writers? Do they have any merit? Or, do these two authors have it wrong?

A recent high-profile case from Canada's armed forces may shed further light on this troubling question.

Subculture in the Military

In 1993, an event unfolded—and I hope I am not being too melodramatic here—that scarred the soul of Canada. Consideration of that event here may help to provide us with a useful context for discussions later in the book. Canada as a country, historically, has taken some pride in the fact that it has contributed to world order and peace by deploying its troops to many parts of the world for peacekeeping duties. Canadian soldiers have been characterized as something approaching angels of mercy and have, more often than not, been honoured and accepted by the citizens of countries in which they were serving.

In 1992-93, Canadian troops were sent to Somalia on a peacekeeping mission. The soldiers were members of the Canadian Airborne Regiment. A subsequent inquiry has discovered that some of these peacekeeping soldiers conducted themselves in a brutal, racist manner and, in fact, tortured and murdered a 16-year-old Somali youth. One disturbing phenomenon that has emerged from the inquiry is that the military has its own entrenched subculture, and that this subculture is often characterized by some of the things Desroches and Grossi and Berg talk about. One of the chief characteristics is the tendency for recruits to allow themselves to "buy into" the subculture in such a way that their loyalty to colleagues can transcend the responsibility they have to think for themselves and to act according to their own moral sense. Indeed, one military police officer admitted that "his investigations were thwarted by soldiers covering up for each other." While giving evidence at the Somali inquiry, this military police officer added: "We're soldiers first and tradesmen second," later suggesting that if he were the one being questioned by the police, he would probably keep quiet as well. (*The Toronto Star*, October 15, 1996, p. A2)

In 1993, on the CBC radio program *Morningside*, during a discussion about the Somali affair between host Peter Gzowski and a retired lieutenant-colonel of the Canadian military, the lieutenant-colonel referred to what she described as the "dangerous bonding" that can take place in military units; this bonding, she claimed, effectively inhibits—if not prohibits—individual moral decision-making. She asserted—and I am paraphrasing here—that the individual (soldier in this case) must constantly be reminded that he continues to carry full responsibility for his moral decision-making irrespective of the prevailing ethos or subculture.

De-individuation

It may be useful to contrast the lieutenant-colonel's point of view with something psychologists call "de-individuation." Psychology professor James Ogloff defines de-individuation thus: "There is pressure exerted by the group and people lose the ability to regulate their individual behaviour." He adds: "You are not held accountable for what has gone on, so you end up doing things you wouldn't do individually." (*Maclean's*, January 30, 1995, p. 18)

It may be difficult, however, to reconcile the lieutenant-colonel's view that individuals continue to carry full responsibility for their actions when, if Ogloff is correct, peer pressure or subcultural constraints can cause individuals to lose the ability to regulate their behaviour. In other words, that in a sense they become victims. (This apparent conundrum would make a lively topic for debate in your class. But let's continue the discussion.)

In a haunting article entitled "Discretion no part of valour" in *The Globe and Mail* (October 1, 1996, p. A6), Eron Main, a former Canadian military officer, refers to the Somalia affair. The article is a confession of sorts. Main writes: "The unofficial military code I lived by involved turning a blind eye to my fellow officers' misdeeds. Ultimately such 'loyalty' led to the Somali inquiry as well as to my retirement." He adds: "We learned the lessons of loyalty a little too well, until we gave it where it was no longer deserved: to the officers who had debased their commissions, and were no longer good and honest." Main, in reflecting on his days as a student at the Royal Military College of Canada, talks about the code of loyalty: "In four years I had encountered many future officers who neglected the college motto—Truth, Duty, Valour—in favour of the unofficial code: Don't Get Caught. I knew of several whom I considered unworthy of their commissions. Of course, I would say nothing. We had been taught from our first day as cadets that we should never, ever, betray our friends, our classmates, our fellow officers."

These sentiments echo many of the thoughts and comments expressed to me by respondents in my dissertation research. They also echo many of the comments made to faculty in our justice department by students when they return to classes after serving their field practica with police forces or in correctional institutions. Now let's try to relate what we have been discussing to justice students and the college classroom.

One of the more difficult challenges I have had to face in my teaching career was dealing with a group of angry justice students who had decided to punish a classmate. The classmate had expressed dismay to a teacher that a number of students had cheated on an examination. Briefly, the teacher, in handing out an examination paper and after instructing the students to leave the papers upside down on their desks, realized she was two papers short. She told the students to leave the papers upside down and she went back to her office to photocopy some extras. While she was gone it appears there was open season on exchange of information by approximately two-thirds of the students! Several minutes later, the teacher returned to a now quiet classroom and instructed the group to turn over their papers and commence writing the examination. One by one the students finished writing the examination and excused themselves from the classroom. The last student to leave was the one I mentioned above. She said to the teacher, thinking there was no other student within earshot: "I have a problem with your leaving the classroom. It allowed several students an opportunity to cheat, and I don't feel that is fair." One of the other students was waiting outside the door and overheard the comment. To shorten a long story, what happened in the next few days was alarming but may come as little or no surprise to many of you reading this account.

Word got out and the reporting student was treated mercilessly by her formerly friendly classmates. On the second day after the incident, she came into my office in a fragile state to declare she could not put up with the hostility anymore. Even though she was in the final term of a two-year program, she had decided to drop out of school. She had committed the cardinal mistake of betraying her classmates. (Perhaps it was Eron Main fearing this kind of reprisal that caused him and his military colleagues to say nothing about the major indiscretions of classmates and colleagues.)

The most sobering thought of all about this event is that these were the same justice students who, the previous semester when we were discussing the notion of subculture in a class, each protested that there would be little or no chance of their ostracizing a colleague for doing the right thing. As discomforting as the examination incident was, and as painful for the student as it was, it provided a useful vehicle for discussion and learning. The student stayed in college, graduated and is doing an excellent job in the corrections field.

Reflections

What do you think about values and attitudes that can be picked up by new recruits to the military, to policing or to corrections?

Should loyalty to colleagues be fostered as an appropriate and, indeed, necessary value? If so, what consequences might inheriting this value have on your ability to make the decisions you—and you alone—feel you must make in the context of your work?

Summary

The primary purpose of this book, as perhaps you can see, is to stimulate you the student to think courageously and deeply about ethical dilemmas. The issue of colleague loyalty above all else, is just one of many that seems to be an integral part of being employed in the justice field. To be able and willing to engage in honest, unbridled discussion of issues like this one demands a high degree of maturity and courage. For you to resist the temptation to react defensively will constitute a distinct challenge. Of course, if you consider the ideas and questions in this book in a mature and honest way, and you are still convinced that the way in which you thought about them originally can be justified, then that is fine. The intention is not necessarily to change your thinking, though that may happen on some issues; it is simply to provide you with an opportunity for considering the issues in a deeper way.

The idea that it is often difficult to remain one's own person in the face of subcultural constraints constitutes a central theme of the book.

Another important purpose is to encourage you to work toward some personal resolution regarding some of the issues raised, where such resolution can be justified. To be able to achieve this, of course, some tools might be helpful to assist in the process. The good news is that some are available and they will be discussed in detail in Chapter 7. Opportunities will be provided for you to practise using these tools as you struggle to reach some conclusions regarding the dilemmas.

The dilemmas offered for discussion are not hypothetical. It is my hope that they will touch a chord in you because of their practical significance. They are real. They have been experienced and recounted to me either by my students while on their field practica, or by officers and administrators of police forces and correctional institutions in Canada and Australia. Some of the specific details I have changed in the interests of ensuring that no police force, correctional institution or individual is identifiable from the information given. Some of the dilemmas are ones more likely to be experienced by police and correctional institution administrators, and others by frontline officers. I would encourage you to "have a go" at thinking your way through both the administrator and officer dilemmas. In this way, you may become more sensitized to the dilemmas others can experience.

Reflections

Should a police force or correctional institution manager encourage subordinate officers to think for themselves?

How do you feel about this idea of thinking for yourself, especially at times when your colleagues may be suggesting strongly that you not do so?

One final note. The fact that the situations included for discussion are *dilemmas* indicates that they probably beg no hard and fast solutions. Indeed, there may well be no one right answer. What we can do is to make a choice that is the best available, while acknowledging that the perfect solution does not exist.

Before we get to the point in the text where these dilemmas are posed, however, you will be aware that chapters 2 and 3 address important topics which, I hope, will become subjects of debate and discussion almost before anything else is discussed in your class. Chapter 2 addresses The Ethics of Teaching Ethics in Justice Programs and Chapter 3, as has been noted, addresses The Role of the Ethics Educator: The Lurking Dangers of Indoctrination. In my experience, it is unusual to encourage students, either in a book like this one or in an ethics course, to participate in a dialogue about these issues. However, discussion of these topics with your instructor will probably be helpful in setting the climate and tone of your classroom experience. It may also help in establishing some parameters.

More important perhaps, it may save you and your instructor some of the pain and anguish my students and I have experienced over the years caused by fuzzy role expectations, unclear teacher intentions, and miscommunication regarding the purpose of the ethics course.

2 The Ethics of Teaching Ethics in Justice Programs

In taking the ethics course, I have now established a better understanding of who I am, what I stand for, and for what reasons.

— *Journal entry. Justice student in ethics course.*

After reading this chapter, you should be able to

- Explain what we mean by **teaching ethics**
- Explain what the purpose of ethics education might be
- Identify reasons for including ethics education in curriculae
- Explain what is meant by **advice-giving** by a teacher
- Identify in what situations advice-giving may be appropriate
- Explain the collaborative approach to ethics education

The Debate over Ethics Education

It may be clear to you from the first chapter that I believe a good case can be made for the wisdom of including ethics courses in justice training programs. This view itself, however, bears some examination, for there are some strong and articulate voices that express reservations about the usefulness of including ethics education in any kind of professional training program or academic course. In the interests of honest enquiry, where all views, values, ideas and opinions are subject to scrutiny, and in the interests of modelling what is being asked of you the reader, it makes sense to include you in a debate about the usefulness of ethics education in preparation for work in the justice field. Keep in mind that what follows is a cursory glance at what various people have to say about this topic. The intent is to offer something that will make you begin thinking about the whole area of ethics education, with the hope that you will follow up with more reading and research of your own as you seek to make your opinions and views informed ones.

The "Teaching" of Ethics

Perhaps an appropriate starting point to the discussion would be to consider what we mean by the phrase "teaching ethics"? Can ethics be taught?

"Teaching ethics" is an unfortunate term, and one that is likely to lead to considerable misunderstanding. Any teacher who teaches ethics, in the strictest sense of the term, would presumably have to be an ethics expert in the sense that she would have to know the right answer to all kinds of moral dilemmas, including dilemmas faced by you and me as individuals. Clearly, it would be a foolish person who would claim to possess this kind of all-encompassing wisdom. Such an expert would also have to know, presumably, which of the tools discussed in Chapter 7 would invariably be successful in enabling us to make "correct" moral decisions. Few people would be likely to lay claim to this kind of expertise. Indeed, it is quite probable that those coming closest to legitimately being able to make such a claim would be the most humble and self-effacing about their expertise. Have you ever noticed how those who are most wise are often the first to question their wisdom, and those who are not wise are often the first to lay claim to wisdom? So, if there is one thing we can probably agree upon in this text, it is that such absolute wisdom is most unlikely to exist. It may be more appropriate to think in terms of a teacher or trainer *facilitating* the ethics educational experience, rather than *teaching* ethics.

Reflections

What do you think about the idea of someone "teaching" you ethics?

John Chandler (1987), professor of ethics, in Martinson's *Discourse on Ethics* talks about reflecting on his role as an ethics professor and his pondering Socrates's question "Can virtue be taught?" He makes a clear distinction between teaching and learning and makes the point that "surely, morality and ethics can be learned....Whether morality can be taught discursively arouses some skepticism in all of us, but certainly there are institutional arrangements by which values can be learned." (p. 9) These "institutional arrangements" would presumably include classes facilitated, if not taught in the traditional sense, by professors. Chandler does not fully explain what he means. In any event, I think the distinction between teaching and learning is a useful one. So, rather than talking in terms of teachers and trainers "teaching ethics," it may be better to talk in terms of teachers providing opportunities for you and other students to think and learn for *yourselves* about ethical decision-making.

One of my students, at the end of an ethics course, wrote in a journal: "What you are doing is helping us understand the practical dimensions of ethics in general and how they relate to specific correctional issues. You are leading the horses (us) to ethical waters. Whether we drink or not is up to us individually."

Another wrote: "I can honestly say that I was quite surprised that you had not overtly attempted (as far as I could tell) to influence our thinking. I thought you would attempt to try this in a way that was discreet and casual."

These comments reflect what the students' experience of an ethics course might be. In other words, that it is important that there always be scope and safety in the classroom for personal choice and personal decision-making.

The Purpose of "Teaching" Ethics

What is the purpose of activities such as discussing and debating ethical issues? Would it be reasonable to assume that if one works in an environment characterized by a "subculture" (discussed briefly in the introductory chapter and discussed in greater depth in chapters 4 and 5), there may be considerable pressure upon an individual to follow the norms of the group in which she works, and to do the accepted thing? If individuals choose not to yield to the subcultural pressures, the penalties can be severe. That being the case, would it again be reasonable to assume (and this is borne out by my research, discussed in the chapters mentioned above) that individuals from time to time may choose to act less ethically than they might do otherwise, simply because they consider the potential costs of doing what they think is the right thing to be too great?

What, then, are justice educators to do, particularly those who are concerned with the ethical aspects of working in corrections or policing? Should they simply inform you the student that this is the way things are, and that the subcultural constraints are a reality which has to be accommodated if you are to survive? Should they ignore this facet of work in this field and allow you to learn about the constraints the hard way? It is my experience that the more common approach is the latter one. Indeed, a quick, informal survey of police education and correctional worker students, and of police officers and correctional officers, indicated that the issue of subcultural constraints generally is not addressed in training programs. Some of these respondents, after my addressing the issue in ethics seminars they were attending, expressed concern in some cases, and anger in others, that this issue had not been addressed.

Reflections

What is your take on this issue? Do you feel that your teachers should tell you about the potentially unpleasant and troubling aspects of working in the justice field?

Should they attempt to heighten your awareness about group pressure and how it can impact on your sense of individual moral responsibility?

If you feel they should, is there any risk that this information may unfairly colour your perception of the job, or lead you toward cynicism even before you get started in your career?

If you feel they should not, and that it is better for you to find out about the troubling parts of the job on your own, might you in some way blame them later on for not fully informing you?

Is There a Place for Ethics Education?

Let's return to the original question: whether there is a place for ethics education in justice training. As was stated earlier there is quite a debate surrounding this issue and there are some equally convincing voices on both sides.

A report issued by the University of Alberta Task Force on Ethics (1985) and a subsequent Progress Review (1988) provide a useful framework for this discussion. They serve as a catalyst for examining some of the various perspectives on ethics education. The original report was based on the results of an extensive survey of opinions of faculty, students and professional associations. The survey results led the university to commit itself to the idea that it should play an active role in ethics education (p. 67 following). Indeed, the first recommendation called for a required exposure to ethics education for all first-year undergraduate students:

> That the University require all first-year undergraduate students to take a course with an ethical component. This need not mean that every student must take one particular course, but may involve a choice from a variety of courses which have been identified as having a significant ethical dimension. (p. 73)

Most important, the report makes it clear that its purpose "is not to promote the instilling of specific ethics, but to raise the level of awareness about ethical issues." (p. 24) This is a critical distinction to make, and it helps us develop a better understanding of the difference between teaching ethics *per se*, and providing an opportunity for learning about ethics and moral decision-making. If I regard my role as one of "teaching ethics," then, as we said earlier, this implies I know best, in which case I would probably wish you to do what I suggest, or tell you, to do. It also raises the ugly possibility of what I call the lurking dangers of indoctrination. This topic is discussed in greater detail in Chapter 3 (see pp. 27 following).

The university survey results are interesting. Eighty-two percent of 1,025 students surveyed agreed that a "university education should help a student develop ethically." (p. 58) The professors' responses were recorded by department, the highest rate of agreement to this concept being found in the faculties of law (91 percent), and health sciences (89 percent). This is encouraging for those of us who feel that one day we may need the services of either a lawyer or a doctor! Or, might it indicate that these are the two professions most in need of ethical attention?

As indicated earlier, and not surprisingly perhaps, there was quite a diversity of opinion expressed by the university professors in their written responses to the survey questions. More often than not, their comments were either completely *for* the teaching of ethics, or they were completely *against* it. This is a topic that seems to attract strong opinions in one direction or the other.

The comments of those opposed to the notion of ethics education are particularly interesting. One respondent noted: "We must be careful about a university trying to shape ethics and morality for the community as a whole, because different people have different conceptions of values and ethics." (pp. 37-38) Another responded: "I don't believe it [the teaching of ethics] should be a goal in itself. The ethics systems of our university-age students are already in place and are basically unalterable at that age." (p. 38) One response was clearly conditioned by the fear of the possibility of indoctrination: "University professors are, other than in intelligence, like the general population, and include some people who lack moral judgement. In God's name, no potted required courses in ethics and values! This results in brainwashing, not critical thinking, in promoting 'acceptable attitudes,' not hard thinking." (p. 38) And finally: "No one becomes ethical merely by teaching or taking a course in ethics. Every course ought to be an ethical exercise." (p. 38)

The caution expressed in the first quote is one worth heeding. As we have indicated, we should take great care not to attempt to legislate a particular concept of morality, or to claim any monopoly on wisdom in this regard.

The second sentiment, adopting the view that students' values are pretty well fixed by university age, is a surprising one. Many people who are involved in any kind of teaching activity with adults speak about the way values can change as a result of the educational process. This would be particularly true of those students who may have simply "adopted" their value system from others, without thinking about those values in any real way. One of my students wrote in a journal: "Before coming into this [Ethics] class I felt that once you reached a certain stage your ethics were set, but because this course has made me look at myself, certain things have changed." And another wrote: "I have learned that my opinions and beliefs are not carved in stone, and may be changed if presented with a good argument."

The third sentiment again is one worth heeding. The legislating of ethics and values by an individual or organization necessarily forecloses on individual critical thinking. The danger here would be that of the individual being required to subjugate his own sense of morality in the interests of fitting in.

The fourth and final sentiment also requires serious consideration. To think of a course in ethics as some kind of panacea for all the ills of a particular justice system would be foolhardy. The view that every facet of a justice program should include consideration of ethical issues seems to be a more appropriate approach.

Nonetheless, most of the opinions in the report were in support of the idea of ethics education in principle, although there was some disagreement as to what form this should take.

Reflections

Are you surprised that 82 percent of the 1,025 students surveyed for the University of Alberta report agreed that the university should help them develop ethically?

What is your view on the opinion expressed by one professor that by the time students are of post-secondary age (generally 18 and up) their values are pretty well set?

One professor is clearly of the view that ethics courses are designed to promote "'acceptable attitudes,' not hard thinking." What do you think of this point of view? (*Note*: This is a question that you could and should be asking yourself at this point in the course *and* at its conclusion).

Two writers in the ethics area, Daniel Callaghan and Sissela Bok (1980), in their discussion of the doubtful goals of teaching ethics, affirm:

> It is often said that one test of the success of teaching ethics would be change in the moral *behaviour* of students, and that a central goal should thus be an attempt to change behaviour....this is an exceedingly dubious goal. First, even if a course could change behaviour, it is hard to see how, short of constant reinforcement of the new behaviour, its effects could be long or surely sustained once out of the classroom; other influences would play their role, and no course could be a permanent antidote against them. (p. 69)

In the justice context, of course, one significant influence would be that of subcultural constraints. And these writers are in all likelihood correct in affirming that it would be highly improbable that an ethics course, in and of itself, could be a permanent antidote for those influences. My own experience of teaching ethics courses and conducting ethics seminars is that they do, indeed, have a "shelf life"; that is, that any effects begin to wear off after a while. Several students have talked to me about the importance of providing what they call "booster shots."

The discussion also raises the issue of the importance of thinking about supplementing ethics courses by encouraging teachers and students to consider the ethical implications of all elements of any educational program in justice departments. Consideration of the ethical dimensions of courses on, for example, Evidence, Arrest Techniques, Court Procedures, Security Techniques, or Use of Force Legislation, to name just a few, could build upon learning and skills developed in a foundation ethics course.

Advice-giving

Is there a place for advice-giving by your teacher in ethics courses? There are those who feel there may be a place for advice-giving so long as it is done carefully and sensitively by a credible and knowledgeable person. One of my teachers at the University of Toronto, in fact, advocated for such a viewpoint. Clive Beck (1991), in *How Adults Learn Values*, wrote:

> People have a strong interest in the outcomes of their behaviour and will adjust their values and actions in the light of information about consequences of behaviour. Much of this information can be made available through instruction. (p. 14)

Michael Davis (1990), in an article entitled "Who Can Teach Workplace Ethics?" takes a similar view. One way of teaching ethics, he claims, is what he calls the "prudence" approach:

> You explain right and wrong in terms of what the employer, the law, or the profession wants and what will happen if one disobeys. You might, for example, explain why an employee should be prompt in this way: 'If you don't want to get fired, arrive on time.' (p. 30)

There may indeed be a place for this kind of prescriptive approach in justice training, because someone who knows the expectations and fully articulates them can save a new officer from considerable grief later. It is particularly important to pass this information on to recruits, because only by so doing could they reasonably be held accountable for subsequent unacceptable behaviour.

It would be important here, of course, to inform students about policies and procedures, the mission statement if there is one, and the "lore" of the institution or the force—the unwritten rules of conduct governing correctional and police officers.

This kind of advice-giving about the rules and expectations of a particular workplace by teachers, however, as important as it is, is not the same as teachers telling you how you should respond to ethical dilemmas you encounter in the course of your job.

The Collaborative Process

Earlier we talked about the role of the teacher in facilitating the ethics educational experience. While there may be a place for teachers prescribing employer expectations in terms of behaviour, it would be more consistent with a facilitative approach to learning for the teacher and student to engage in a collaborative process. This approach would be characterized by the teacher being both a teacher and a learner, and the student also being both a teacher and a learner. Clive Beck (1991), in *Approaches to Values Education*, says:

> ...a large proportion of the teaching is done by the learners, who instruct each other and their 'teacher'. The main point of values instruction, therefore, is not that one person tells other people what to value, but rather that there is explicit, systematic, joint enquiry into value matters. (p. 8)

In the business context, Dan Rice and Craig Dreilinger (1990) also favour the collaborative approach. The ethics experience, they affirm, should accomplish three goals: a) heighten employees' ethical awareness; b) provide them with the means to identify ethical issues; and c) help them develop tools to clarify and resolve ethical issues. (p. 106) There is no hint of "telling" or prescriptiveness in this view; the approach is one characterized by cooperation and helping on the part of the "teacher."

One of the reasons we should be careful about an overly prescriptive approach to ethics education is that as human beings we are each unique. Therefore, each of us necessarily brings to any moral dilemma subjective perspectives. Nel Noddings (1984), in her book *Caring: A Feminine Approach to Ethics and Moral Education*, talks about the "uniqueness of human encounters including those in the moral domain." (p. 5) She adds:

Since so much depends on the subjective experience of those involved in ethical encounters, conditions are rarely 'sufficiently similar for me to declare that you must do what I must do.' (p. 5)

And Daniel Callaghan and Sissela Bok (1980), whom we mentioned earlier, in a book they edited called *Ethics Teaching in Higher Education*, also caution against a "telling" approach:

No teacher of ethics can assume that he or she has such a solid grasp on the nature of morality as to pretend to know what finally counts as good moral conduct....It is the time and place to teach them [students] intellectual independence, and to instill in them a spirit of critical enquiry. (p. 71)

Reflections

What are your views about having a separate "foundation" course in ethics, supported by you and your teachers, considering the ethical dimensions and implications of all your program courses?

Is there a place for advice-giving by your teacher in the context of an ethics course? If so, what kind of advice would you a) expect to be given, and b) feel okay about being given? If you feel there is no place for advice-giving by the teacher, why not?

In the context of a justice program, do you think there is a place for a collaborative approach to learning between you and your teacher?

Summary

We have discussed whether there is a place for ethics education in justice training. We have suggested that because of police and corrections subcultural constraints on the autonomy of the individual, for these people taking time out for thought and reflection about ethical issues and moral dilemmas might be an important and wise use of time. We have suggested that stand-alone ethics courses lose much of their potential effectiveness if attention is not also paid to the ethical implications of all aspects of a justice training curriculum. We have suggested that the role of the teacher is an important one, but that how it is played out deserves some attention. We have suggested that there may be a place for advice-giving on the part of the knowledgeable and experienced teacher but that this should be engaged in cautiously. And finally, we have suggested that a collaborative approach to learning in an ethics course might be the less problematic approach in terms of negating the potential effects of teacher influence.

In the chapter following, we will consider this latter point in greater detail.

The Role of the Ethics Educator: The Lurking Dangers of Indoctrination

I sometimes found your mannerism was downright frustrating, because you did not help us make right choices.... You helped prepare us for possible situations we might encounter, and the dilemmas we might face in those encounters.

— Journal entry. Justice student in ethics course.

During the course a lot was said about teaching ethics and being influential. I don't think a person can teach ethics and not be influential.

— Journal entry. Justice student in ethics course.

I believe that a teacher has just as much of a right in stating his or her opinion and thoughts on any issue, as long as the students are aware that all people have this right.   *— Journal entry. Justice student in ethics course.*

I was sure that this course was meant to change my opinions and my beliefs. I also thought that you, the professor, thought your ethics were the correct ones, and planned to force them on us. However, something changed along the way and I began to realize there are two sides to every issue. Maybe my opinion wasn't always the right one.   *— Journal entry. Justice student in ethics course.*

After reading this chapter, you should be able to

- *Identify and explain some dangers with respect to the role of the ethics educator*
- *Describe the notion of **teacher influence***
- *Explain why the teacher-student dynamic is a particularly awkward one in the context of ethics education*
- *Identify at least one reason why students sometimes do not trust a teacher's invitation for them to think critically and independently*
- *Identify four characteristics of critical thinkers*

The Worry about Indoctrination

You may wonder why, in a book like this one that has been written for students like you, I have included a discussion on the role of the ethics educator. Let me explain.

Many ethics educators worry about the potential for their becoming doctrinaire in their approach to ethics education or for being perceived by their students to be so. This is a legitimate concern. That what I do in the ethics classroom will be perceived by my students as indoctrinatory has caused me some angst over the last 17 years since I started teaching ethics courses. The word "angst" is used advisedly. Much of the discussion that follows is based on my own personal experience and struggle. My hope is that this discussion and debate will provide interesting and provocative food for thought in your classroom. I would suggest that you think deeply about this important topic, and I would also encourage you to be as honest about it as you can be in any classroom discussion.

Clearly, my discomfort would seem to indicate that I see the words "indoctrinate" or "doctrinaire" as necessarily negative ones. I consider a doctrinaire approach one to be avoided studiously. Perhaps I should explain here, without getting into too much of a philosophical discussion, what I mean by "indoctrinate." What I mean by the notion, first, is the attempt by one person (teacher in this case) to get another person or persons (students) to accept a particular position. Included in the notion, second, would be the intention by the teacher to withhold from a student the opportunity and right to consider that position for herself, and to develop her own perspective on it.

Instinctively I feel that there is something improper or inappropriate about one adult, especially one in a position of power as would be the case with a teacher, imposing on adults his views on various moral issues.

However, I have to confess that a significant problem for me is that I tend to hold strong personal views on some of the moral issues I discuss with my students. That is not to say I am inflexible; indeed, over the years I have come to accept different perspectives on many of the issues discussed because of the contribution of my students. On other issues, however, nothing that has been said by others has influenced my thinking. That being the case, it is a source of concern for me that some of my stronger views may in some way "leak out" during discussions with students.

Should an Ethics Educator "Come Clean" About Her Values?

It should be noted, of course, that some ethicists and educators feel that laying one's own views on the table is an appropriate and necessary thing to do. The knack, they claim, is to ensure that one's students are made to feel no pressure to accept those views and are encouraged to express alternative ones. Indeed, some are of the view that to refrain from doing so may be dishonest or manipulative.

A philosophy professor, during one of my postgraduate courses at university, used this technique of stating his views on each topic prior to class discussion. As a student, I was taken aback when he led off each discussion by arguing forcibly for his own view. I asked him whether he felt there was any danger of his foreclosing on dissenting student views because as the professor and the awarder of grades he might intimidate students. Did he feel students might feel obliged to acquiesce to his point of view? His response was that it was his responsibility to "come clean" about his own views, put them on the table, get them out in the open—but then work to create an atmosphere where students would feel comfortable in attacking those views if they could.

I am not entirely convinced. There! I have expressed a personal opinion on this issue. There is a distinct danger, in my view, whether one is a professor, or a staff trainer at a police or corrections training academy, of being perceived to be overly influential on the group. The teacher is invariably going to be seen by the students, and with some justification, to be in a position of power, and this is going to be an ever-present dynamic in the classroom. This potential for influence may be less of a problem at the postgraduate level, but it is still there; and at lower levels of education it is going to be very much there.

During one class with this particular professor I gathered up my courage and expressed surprise at his approach. Surely, it is a risky activity to argue his own views? Surely, it would be more appropriate to attempt to minimize, in whatever way he can, his potential for influencing his students? During the discussion, one classmate gently reminded me that, as laudible as it was that I was concerned about the dangers of too much influence over the thinking of others, it was inevitable. It was pointed out to me that the fact that I am male, white, speak with a British accent, and may be perceived by students as something of an expert, I can operate from no position other than one of power. Try as a teacher might, therefore, it can be extremely difficult to create a climate of open, honest debate with his students, whether he comes clean about his views or not.

Perhaps at this point it would help the dialogue if we were to examine one of the ethical issues I discuss with my students. The issue is whether it is ethical for an employee to take a "sick day" when he is not sick. This is a particularly contentious issue that inspires some lively discussion in my classes. It is also an issue about which I hold some strong views. Simply put, I feel it is unethical for employees to take a sick day for any reason other than sickness. This is *my* value and it governs my behaviour with respect to this issue. This is not to say that I am correct or that I have not and do not consider other perspectives. Frankly, however, my belief is that for me to take a sick day when I am not sick is tantamount to theft. And, other than for the obvious legal difference, I see little or no moral difference between taking a sick day when I am well and helping myself out of petty cash to whatever I am paid for a day's work.

Students tend to become defensive when we discuss this issue. They often engage in what I consider to be rationalizing. Sick days, they argue, are provided for in the employment contract and they are an employee's right. Who is to say what sickness is or what it is not? What if, despite my not being sick, I come back to work the following day and perform better as a result? All kinds of what I consider to be red herrings are drawn across the trail. Participants tend to struggle for a reasonable and defensible response when it is suggested to them that such provisions in the contract are there in case there is a genuine need to use them; that the sick day provision is made for *bona fide* cases of sickness.

The challenge for me—and I constantly question myself about this—is whether given my strong feelings on this issue, and even though I do not express an opinion on the issue, it is possible for me to intellectually challenge others' ideas and perspectives in a dispassionate way? *It is this sort of question that is kernel to worries about indoctrination.* Not only am I a person holding power, but I am also a person holding strong views on certain important issues. We need to ask ourselves whether these are, potentially if not actually, two active ingredients in the indoctrination process.

What if, hypothetically, my views can be demonstrated to be morally sound? Does this give me the right to influence or attempt to influence the views of others; in other words, to have their thinking become more akin to mine? Is the role of the ethics educator one of deliberately setting out to make individuals more ethical; to have them think and act in a way prescribed by the educator? Or, is it more the mutual engaging in a process of critical thinking about, and examination of issues?

Let's say for the moment that the latter question reflects more accurately what should be going on in an ethics classroom; that you the students are encouraged to think critically and to think for yourselves. Might there, however, still be a possibility of the ethics educator, especially one who is well-liked by you, of seducing you into thinking in a given way? If the learning climate is a comfortable one, where the teacher is respected, trusted and well-liked, might this be fertile ground for the overt or covert manipulation of your group to that teacher's own views? Let's consider another example.

Later in the book, reference is made to a conversation I had with a student when I was administrator of the justice department at the college where I work. The student was in the police education program and he had been caught cheating on an examination. When I asked him how he would square this activity of cheating with the trust and responsibility society would invest in him as a police officer, his reply was, "It would be different if I were in uniform, I would be honest on the job." Several years later I am still trying to come to terms with this response and the kind of thinking and morality that would inspire it. The student clearly felt that it was okay to be dishonest in one's personal life, but not in one's professional life. There appears to be little or no cognition of the possibility that the two may have some kind of connection.

This incident is often a topic of discussion in my classes. It is common for participants to defend this student's response. What we have here then is a situation where, in a real sense, I would like the participants to see that there may be something worrying about the student's response—in other words, to come around to my way of thinking. As a result of the debate and the concerns I raise, some may change their thinking and come to see that perhaps there *is* something worrying about the student's response.

What has happened here? Have I been guilty of indoctrination? Or, have I simply been an agent of change for those who have decided for themselves to embrace the change? Certainly, no one is prohibited from, or judged for, continuing to think in any way she chooses on the issue. The students are challenged intellectually, and are asked to offer reasons for their views. And even if they can't defend their views they are still, of course, free to continue holding them, unreasoned and contradictory as they may appear to be.

Comfort can be taken from the fact that wishing students would embrace a view I hold strongly may not be the same as inducing that embracing by way of psychological coercion or by overt or covert suppression of different ways of thinking. But the issues of power and control on the part of the teacher remain, and in my view need to be constantly guarded against. Sociologist Kimberley Folse (1991), in a journal article entitled "Ethics and the Profession: Graduate Student Training," refers to Churchill (1982), who makes the point that "moral values cannot fail to be taught" by teachers (p. 306). If this view has any merit, teachers find themselves in an unenviable position, through no fault of their own. It is as though they have had this (unwanted) mantle of responsibility placed upon them.

Reflections

Should a teacher, particularly in an ethics course, be worried about being—or being perceived to be—doctrinaire by his students?

Would you prefer your ethics teacher to "come clean" about her personal views on a topic under discussion, or attempt to conceal them?

With respect to guarding against teacher influence, what do you think is the responsibility of the ethics teacher when one student says in class, "I think the trouble with this country is Chinamen and Pakis (sic)," or another says, "Aboriginal people are given too much money by this government, and they are all a bunch of drunken bums?"

Is there a place in the classroom for teacher influence if it is exercised in the challenging of racist or sexist remarks?

To what extent, if any, should teachers attempt to influence students who exhibit socially unacceptable attitudes?

If you think there is a place for a teacher to challenge socially unacceptable opinions, might this get in the way of the teacher being able to create an open climate where students feel they can state what they truly feel on a given topic?

What is your experience with respect to teachers and how they can influence you?

The Teacher-Student Dynamic in Ethics Education

As we have suggested, because of their role teachers necessarily find themselves in positions of power. They are in a unique position to influence. The potential for influence generally has its roots in either the student's fear of, or respect for, the teacher, or simply in the fact that how well the student does in the course is perceived by the student to be in the teacher's hands.

The teacher-student dynamic is a particularly awkward one in the context of ethics education because of the natural propensity of students to see teachers of any subject as experts. Often the relationship, somewhat sadly, is one characterized by the student seeking to "give back to the teacher what the teacher wants." Sometimes this may stem from the student's respect for the teacher's expertise, but more often it stems from the view that if one feeds back to the teacher what the teacher has given out, this is the best way to ensure a good grade. One of the more disappointing moments for me in working with students is for someone to approach me to find out what I "want" on an examination or in an essay. Such enquiries indicate that I have been unable to convey to the student that what I am really interested in is what *they* are thinking about a given topic.

It is a significant challenge, in my experience, to create a safe climate in a classroom where students feel they do not have to worry about agendas—including hidden ones—that the teacher may or may not have. In an effort to combat this fear, I commence any ethics seminar by informing the students that I make an honest attempt to harbour no agenda, hidden or otherwise; I attempt to convey to them that the classroom is a safe forum for the sharing of ideas, and that there are probably going to be no right or wrong answers regarding the issues raised. In other words, that the process of airing and exploring ideas is the important thing.

Traditional Education and Student Conditioning

The problem is that this kind of educational approach in which students are encouraged to think for themselves generally flies in the face of virtually all their previous educational experience. It is generally such an atypical educational approach that they can become suspicious of it, and some even intimidated by it. They have become so used to seeking and finding answers in the classroom that even if one asserts this is not part of the process here, they feel that this is what the teacher is about. Often they feel, probably because of the conditioning that has gone on in many classrooms during the previous 15 years or so, that perhaps in a subterraneous or devious way, the intention is to attempt to lead them to think in a particular way. Often, attempts to disavow them of this notion fall on deaf ears or are met with a reluctance on their part to accept what the teacher is saying.

Leo Buscaglia, the American university teacher who has made a name for himself talking about "love," graphically depicts the problem with teacher-centered education in the foreword to his book *Love*. "Education," he says, "should be the process of helping everyone discover his uniqueness....But we still see the processes again and again of trying to make everyone like everybody else." He continues:

> A few years ago with some of my student teachers at the University, I went back into classrooms and was astounded to find the same things going on that had been going on when I was in school—a million years ago. For example, the art teacher would come in. Remember how we always anticipated and got ready for the art teacher? You put your papers down and you got your Crayolas out and you waited and finally in would walk this harried person. I really feel sorry for an itinerant art teacher. She comes racing in from another class and has time only to nod to the teacher, turn around, and say, "Boys and girls, today we are going to draw a tree." She goes to the blackboard, and she draws *her* tree which is a big green ball with a little brown base. Remember those lollipop trees? I never saw a tree that looked like that in my life, but she put it up there, and she says, "All right, boys and girls, draw." Everybody gets busy and draws.
>
> If you have any sense, even at that early age, you realize that what she really wanted was for you to draw *her* tree, because the closer you got to her tree, the better your grade. (pp. 20-21)

Buscaglia goes on to express concern about this tendency to demand conformity in the classroom, which, he says, continues "right on into the university." "We don't say to people, 'Fly, Think for yourselves.' We give them our old knowledge, and we say to them, 'Now this is what is essential. This is what is important.'"

If Buscaglia is correct, educators should not be surprised if students come into the classroom thinking that academic success depends on the degree to which they conform to the teacher's expectations. Presumably, this requirement to conform would apply to an even greater extent in police and corrections training academies because of the paramilitary nature of many of these facilities.

Is It Possible to Overcome Student Conditioning?

My experience is that there are ways to minimize these suspicions, but I have found that it is not possible to eradicate them. Of course, there are always students who, for whatever reason, seem to be more or less amenable to the new approach. Then there are those who, despite one's protests, continue to feel that the purpose of the exercise is to get them to think in prescribed ways; in other words, that the real purpose is to indoctrinate them.

For example, one of my students wrote:

> During the course a lot was said about teaching ethics and being influential. I don't think a person can teach ethics and not be influential.

And another student, in response to the different, more open, approach to learning, said:

> There is no way that a lifetime of conditioning [concerning previous classroom experiences] can be changed within a semester....

Perhaps a more sobering comment is this one:

> You are well-liked and held with great respect. I feel that people were afraid to say what they felt because they didn't want to lose your respect. In the back of our minds we knew this was wrong and you would never do it, but because of our conditioning through school, that was always in the back of our minds.

The latter comment is one that gives cause for concern for the educator, but it also provides, in a reverse way, a glimmer of optimism. The student who wrote the comment, a) was able to express the concern, and b) felt free enough to sign her name.

Here are some other student journal comments for you to think about:

> If the teacher did put his opinion into the conversation, I feel it would be a bad thing because some students would conform to his values and beliefs.

> There was never a time when the teacher was overly influential. At times he seemed to be concerned by the way certain individuals were thinking, but he never really judged us as unethical. Overall, I think the teacher was influential to the extent that that's what teachers are for—to be of some influence, to help us learn.

> If there was any time that the teacher was influential upon students, it was in their best interests. I think this is all right because he knows what we are going to be getting into and has already experienced it first-hand. He is only trying to prepare us to be successful.

> I was sure that this course was meant to change my opinions and my beliefs. I also thought that you, the professor, thought that your ethics were the correct ones, and that you planned to force your ethics on us. However, something changed along the way and I began to realize there are two sides to every issue.

Reflections

It would seem from these comments that despite my protests, I was only half successful in attempting to neutralize my influence over the students. What do you now think about this awkward and somewhat complex issue of teacher influence?

The Importance of Looking at All Sides

On the surface, what I seek to achieve in my interaction with students is to open their minds to alternative points of view on a given topic, where they are required to consider many sides of the issue before coming to a conclusion. Richard Paul (1992), who is a North American expert on critical thinking, in a chapter entitled "Ethics Without Indoctrination," argues that ethics can and ought to be taught, "but only in conjunction with critical thinking." (p. 240) He goes on to assert that in order to teach ethics morally, the course should be taught in such a way that students become "as adept in using critical thinking principles in the moral domain as we expect them to be in the scientific and social domains of learning." (p. 243) I agree. In my courses I spend time covering some of the principles and skills of critical thinking. I do so for two reasons: a) I agree with Paul that it would be unethical to attempt to teach ethics to individuals when they are unlikely to have the capacity or permission to sort through the arguments themselves, and b) it is a small but significant step toward guarding against the lurking dangers of indoctrination or the perception of indoctrination. The teaching of critical thinking, however, is more successful in protecting against actual indoctrination by the teacher than it is in protecting against the *perception* of indoctrination. Almost invariably, in my view, there will be students who, despite the teacher's best efforts, will become or will continue to be suspicious of the ethics educator's motives.

Here are a few brief comments made by three of my students about the importance of critical thinking. They are included for discussion purposes. The first one calls into question the idea that the educational process should be one that requires the teacher, as expert, to provide facts and information, and the student, in order to be successful, to simply regurgitate this material in examinations or papers:

> I have always had the notion that we never truly think while we are in college. All we do is memorize.

The second comment, even though it is expressed in the way that baseball manager Yogi Berra might have expressed it, contains an idea worth heeding:

> I did find the critical thinking part quite interesting, because it goes to show how much thought we don't put into our thinking.

And:

> It is easy to accept the *status quo* so as to not rock the boat. However, if throughout history no one thought critically about various policies and issues, and had not the courage to ask 'why?', we might still be in the Dark Ages.

Indeed, had no-one had the courage to think critically, perhaps we would still be convinced that the earth was flat, or that it was impossible for humans to fly.

Dialogue

Let's return to the indoctrination worry. Clive Beck (1991), one of my teachers referred to earlier, stresses the importance of dialogue in ethics education, and he sees this approach as one way of avoiding the possibility of the teacher being accused of being doctrinaire. He does caution, however, that: "Even with the dialogue format, authoritarianism may continue." (p. 3) He continues: "Careful planning and constant vigilance are needed to ensure that learners have freedom of speech, belief, and action and that the influence is reciprocal." (p. 3) Borrowing from Freire (1988) and Habermas (quoted in White, 1988), he lists the key elements of dialogue:

a. Respect for each other's insights

b. Respect for each other's 'tradition' or 'story'

c. Shared control of the form and content of dialogue

d. Focus on concrete, lived experience

e. Testing through action (p. 2)

Noted sociologist Max Weber (1967), however, would probably argue that this vigilance against the dangers of indoctrination would not be a sufficient safeguard. He was writing in the context of science education, but one can only assume that his forebodings would be even greater in the ethics education context. He warns of the perils of teachers taking a stand on issues. For example, of political debate he says:

> They [words] are not ploughshares to loosen the soil of contemplative thought; they are swords against the enemies: such words are weapons. It would be an outrage, however, to use words in this fashion in a lecture or the lecture room....But the true teacher will beware of imposing from the platform any political position upon the student. (pp. 145-146)

He becomes almost strident in warning teachers off attempting to answer, or being drawn into, what he calls "questions of the value of culture" in their professional role. (p. 146) "The task of the teacher," he affirms, "is to serve the students with his knowledge and scientific experience, and not to imprint upon them his personal views." (p. 146)

Other Views on the Educator's Role

Two writers and researchers who have written extensively on ethics, Daniel Callaghan and Sissela Bok (1980), have some interesting things to say about this subject. Ethics courses, and by implication ethics teachers, they claim, "should make a change in the way students *think* about ethical issues...by providing them with the tools for a more articulate and consistent means of justifying their moral judgements." (p. 70) One of these tools would be the ability to think clearly, constructively and well. (A discussion of this particular tool and others follows in Chapter 5).

And Jonathon Baron (1990), in a journal article called "Thinking About Consequences," makes an interesting point about the importance of moral thinking:

Much of what we call immoral behaviour, such as the behaviour of Hitler's follow-ers, or less insidiously, the followers of Colonel Oliver North, arose not so much out of malice but rather out of *thoughtlessness*, that is, *failure to think of consequences and relevant moral principles, or out of unreflective commitment to questionable ide-ologies.* (p. 77) [emphasis is mine].

Baron believes not only that there is a place for moral education, but that it is absolutely vital if we are going to develop students with the capacity to think for themselves about ethical issues and moral dilemmas encountered in their per-sonal and professional lives.

One of the ethics teacher's responsibilities would therefore be to ensure that her students are encouraged to do their own critical thinking. It is important that students understand clearly the differences between critical and uncritical think-ing. For example, I advise my students that critical thinkers

- tend not to jump to conclusions;
- examine the credibility of the evidence presented;
- are humble and fair-minded; and
- courageously face up to, and incorporate into their thinking alternative points of view if, after examination, these appear to be credible.

Uncritical thinkers, I tell them, tend to think and act in the opposite way.

Reflections

How would you describe your educational experience up until now? Have you, general-ly, been encouraged by your teachers to think for yourself?

What do you think about the differences between critical and uncritical thinkers? Where do you see yourself in this respect?

How do you respond to the views quoted from the journals of my students?

Would you agree, based on the student comments, that I was only half successful in my attempt to neutralize the potential for influencing my students?

What might be the implications of this partial failure on my part for your experience in an ethics course?

Do you consider yourself—generally, based on the brief references to critical thinking above—to be a critical or uncritical thinker?

Summary

How can we sum up this discussion about the role of the ethics educator?

We have discussed the worry about a doctrinaire approach to ethics education. We have discussed whether it is wise, or appropriate, for the ethics educator to "come clean" about his own views on a discussion topic. We have raised the question of whether it is possible for a teacher who chooses not to express her opinions to conduct a dialogue with students in a dispassionate way. Also raised was the dilemma for the teacher in establishing a safe, open climate for learning, while at the same time challenging socially unacceptable values. We also discussed the challenge that the ethics educator faces in creating a safe learning climate given to independent and critical thinking by his students, when most of the educational conditioning to date is characterized by the notions "teacher knows best" or "teacher as expert."

4 Subculture and the Individual Officer

So you either fit in, or you don't fit in. If you don't fit in you are not going to last. It's the same as the criminal subculture. — *Justice student after field practicum.*

One thing that really scared me was the need for acceptance within the group, which often leads to betraying your own sense of self, and the values we hold.

— *Justice student after field practicum.*

The big dilemma was, do you stand alone and become a leper or do you let peer pressure and group think compromise your ethical stand?

— *Justice student after field practicum.*

There is a price tag attached to honesty, especially in corrections. That is a scary thought. That even though you may be right, and that the actions of a fellow employee may have been wrong, in a subculture it is better to button up than to open up and speak to someone and risk being an outcast.

— *Justice student after field practicum.*

After reading this chapter, you should be able to

- Explain the significance of including a discussion of subculture in a book about ethics
- Explain what we mean by the terms **subculture** and **subcultural constraints**
- List six norms that characterize police and correctional officer subculture
- Identify two of the more significant norms in police and correctional officer subculture
- Explain why police and corrections subcultural norms may be more compelling on officers than subcultural norms in most other workplaces

The Idea of Police and Correctional Officer Subculture

As you will have noticed, the first three chapters referred to the idea of police and correctional officer subculture. I have also alluded to the idea that subcultural constraints may inhibit individual officers from making their own independent, moral decisions. It is because of this latter sentiment that I believe any text addressing ethical issues in the justice field would be incomplete without also addressing one of the more constraining forces against individual moral decision-making—namely, that of a subculture.

In this chapter we will more closely examine the idea of a subculture as it pertains to police and correctional officers. What is a subculture? Is there a difference between a subculture in the justice context and a subculture in other work contexts? What are its defining characteristics?

The discussion in this chapter and the next may touch a nerve. It has the potential to make you feel defensive. On the other hand, some of you may even feel a sense of relief that someone (stupid enough?) like me is prepared to broach the subject!

For you to keep an open mind about this topic, and for you to give it a fair hearing, will require considerable courage, and intellectual and emotional maturity. Of course, if after reading chapters 4 and 5, and thinking about and discussing their contents, you wish to discount some or all of the ideas, then that is, of course, your right. What matters most is what you think. But be aware, it will not be easy for you to keep an open mind. I suspect, based on discussions of this topic with students, that it may be much easier for you to react defensively.

What Do We Mean by "Subculture" and "Subcultural Constraints"?

To help us develop a better understanding of the terms "subculture" and "subcultural constraints," we will consider three sources of information. First, we will turn to a dictionary definition for help. Second, we will discuss the ideas that some faculty members in college justice programs have about these two terms. Third, we will look briefly at what some researchers have to say about them. In the following chapter, we will consider the views of some justice educators, police and correctional officers, and administrators.

First, let's look at a dictionary definition of subculture. The *Collins English Dictionary* (Third Edition) defines subculture as "a subdivision of a national culture or an enclave within it with a distinct integrated network of behaviour, beliefs, and attitudes." The key idea here is that a subculture is characterized by a code of behaviour governed by a set of beliefs and attitudes.

Second, let's consider what faculty in college justice programs have to offer in helping us understand these terms. It is significant, I think, that all of these faculty members have enjoyed careers in the justice field, and since becoming educators have supervised students extensively on their field practica. This activity has enabled these teachers to keep up with developments in the field. It would be reasonable to assume, therefore, that their opinions continue to be current and informed.

The faculty opinions were expressed in a survey that I conducted. Faculty were asked to respond to the question "What do you mean by the term 'subculture'?" Their responses, I believe, were interesting and informative and will provide stimulating topics of discussion for you and your class colleagues. Keep in mind that in all cases the faculty were defining subculture as it relates to the justice field. (In the next chapter we will consider what these justice educators said to me about this topic in one-on-one interviews.)

As you read this chapter, take some time to reflect on your own personal experience. What you think and feel about your workplace and how it impacts upon you as an individual is of critical importance to your development as a human being and as a police or correctional officer.

Here are some samples of survey responses. One teacher wrote: "By subculture, I mean a different, distinct, and separate cultural phenomenon—a culture other than the mainstream culture. One with its own values, beliefs, mores. The major value of this subculture is to 'protect your own butt', and, secondarily, 'to protect and stand by your co-workers.'"

It is interesting to note what this person claims are the two main values characterizing police and correctional officer subculture. Clearly, these two values more often than not characterize *any* workplace. The difference, however, between say, a justice workplace and an automotive plant or an insurance office, may be the *degree* to which these norms characterize those particular workplaces. As we shall see later in this chapter, arguments can be made that because of issues around the safety and security of officers in the justice field, the requirement to adhere to subcultural norms may be stronger.

"The subculture," claims another faculty member, "consists of a set of beliefs, habits, attitudes, and even schemes which determine in large part what line workers [officers] have to do to survive in their occupational environment." Interestingly, this person added in his response that in such a subculture these beliefs and attitudes are conveyed *informally*. They constitute essentially what is a code of conduct for officers, known by all officers but normally not formally communicated. The code becomes understood, almost by osmosis, and then is reinforced when a non-conforming officer is chastised (ostracised?) by her colleagues. We referred in Chapter 1 to the view of Professor Frederick Desroches that "novices [new police officers] entering the group are confronted…with a set of norms and values to which they are exposed and are expected to conform." There are some clear connections here between this particular faculty member's ideas and those of Desroches. The faculty member talks in terms of what "officers have to do," and Desroches talks about an expectation of new officers to conform to what we sometimes call a code of conduct. Both these people make it sound as though one doesn't have much choice in the matter. Perhaps, as we noted in Chapter 1, that is why two researchers, Grossi and Berg (1991), talked in terms of correctional officers having to "compromise their personal values and interests." If this kind of thinking has any merit, isn't it curious that an informal code can be so powerful?

We have referred to an unwritten, informal code of conduct governed by a set of expectations. One faculty member, in explaining his views on subculture, talked in terms of "a group of persons who adhere to an unwritten code of conduct which governs certain areas of behaviour. The subculture is also the vehicle through which values and morals are conveyed by their proponents, and the rewards/punishments imposed for conformity/non-conformity."

Many other faculty members responded in a similar vein to the survey question asking them to define what they mean by "subculture." A recurring theme was that a subculture is generally characterized by expectations that the group has regarding the behaviour of its members.

Third, many of the researchers in this area tend to agree with this kind of thinking. Sociologist Theodore Mills (1967), for example, talked about the norms of the group being "ideas in the minds of members (of that group) about what should or should not be done by a specific member under specified circumstances." (p. 74) Three other researchers—Alan Coffey, Edward Eldefonso and Walter Hartinger (1982)—in discussing police subculture, defined it "as a kind of shorthand term for the organized sum of police perspectives, relevant to the police role." (p. 141) Two others, Darwin Cartwright and Alvin Zander (1968), talk about the pressure that groups can bring to bear on their members: "But it is clear that groups can, and often do, apply pressure on their members, so as to bring about a uniformity of beliefs, attitudes, values, and behaviour....If a cohesive group has developed a standard or a norm, it may exert strong pressures on any member who attempts to deviate." (p. 145)

Perhaps you will agree, if any of the foregoing ideas are worthy of serious consideration, that a discussion of subcultural constraints has a place in a book about ethics. If the group to which we belong, in the interests of maintaining group solidarity, expects us, even occasionally, to give up our right to make our own moral decisions, maybe we should be concerned.

Of course, there are many other aspects of the development of a subculture that need to be taken into consideration, and again the researchers can help us develop an understanding of these.

Some researchers express the view that for a subculture to become established, the subcultural group has to be anti-something or another. In other words, that there has to be a common "enemy." Members of the group join together in their opposition to the "enemy" and this, in turn, can produce the effect of galvanizing the group. For example, sociologist G.L. Webb (1978), in addressing correctional officer subculture, talks about that particular group being anti-inmate, anti-administration and anti-prison social worker. Criminologists Elizabeth Grossi and Bruce Berg (1991) talk about "hostility directed at officers by inmates, their [inmate] families, and often even the public," thereby making them the "enemy."

In the police context, similar sentiments have been expressed by other researchers, including Bittner (1980) and Goldstein (1990). Police officers, for example, when they perceive themselves to be under siege from the public over an alleged act of professional misconduct, often see themselves as being misunderstood. In other words, they feel only a police officer can understand police conduct—"they" (the public) do not understand "us." In the following chapter there is a discussion of one former police officer's description of what he calls the "musk ox syndrome." His depiction graphically portrays how members of a police force may react in the face of public scrutiny or criticism. It doesn't constitute a quantum leap, I think, to see how this kind of dynamic can have the effect of galvanizing a group.

In summary, then, we have briefly examined what we mean by a subculture in the justice field. We have suggested that it is characterized by a set of norms, communicated informally *to* all its members *by* members. These norms are said to govern the conduct of those members if they wish to preserve their membership in the group. We have also discussed the idea of a subcultural group needing—for its formation and continuing existence—to have a real or perceived enemy. We have suggested that this can galvanize the members of the group into a "solid" entity. In the case of police and correctional officers, the "enemy" is often seen to be the criminal element, the officers' respective administrative groups and, perhaps to a lesser degree, the public.

Reflections

Would you agree that the issue of police and correctional officer subculture is a highly sensitive and emotive one? If so, why do you think this is so? What feelings have you been having since you began thinking about the topic?

How would you define "subculture" in the justice context to someone who had no idea what you were talking about?

What are your views on the idea of an unwritten code of conduct governing the behaviour of police and correctional officers at work?

Is There a Difference Between Correctional and Police Officer Subculture, and Subculture in Other Workplaces?

You will have noticed, for the purposes of this book, that the notions of "police officer subculture" and "correctional officer subculture" are used interchangeably as though they are, to a large extent, one and the same thing.

More research has been done on the former so we know a little more about subculture in the police context. From this research it may be argued that the subculture in policing is stronger than it is in correctional institutions, and that the influence of the subculture tends to remain relatively constant across differing police authorities. The idea of a police brotherhood is believed by most to extend across police departments. Perhaps that is why in countries like Canada, the U.S.A., Australia and Britain, to name a few, it is customary in sad instances of a police officer fatality for officers from other forces to attend the funeral to express support and solidarity. It is also common for correctional officers to send delegates to such funerals.

With respect to corrections, my research indicates that the strength of the subculture tends to correlate with the security level of a correctional facility. It tends to be strongest in maximum security institutions, and becomes weaker as the security level is reduced. However, even in minimum security institutions, an officer subculture is still evident, although the constraints are generally not as strictly enforced. For example, it is conceivable that officers working in minimum security facilities may see the inmate population not so much as the "enemy" but as a group of individuals who may benefit from their incarceration. Generally, this is most unlikely to be the case in maximum security institutions, and somewhat less likely to be the case in medium security facilities. This view was borne out in a discussion I had with an institution administrator. He said: "The nature of the subculture and how ingrained it is, in my opinion, depends on whether you are in maximum security, medium security, or minimum security. It is just like the inmate subculture which is highly ingrained in maximum, less so in medium, and less in minimum."

That having been said, police and correctional officer subcultures share, in my view, a number of common characteristics. These allow us to regard them as sufficiently similar to warrant considering them together. For the sake of simplification, then, and to avoid the risk of becoming bogged down in a debate over the finer differences between police and correctional officer subculture, or over the differences between subculture in a maximum security setting and a less secure institution setting, we will consider them to be essentially similar.

There may be a place in another book for a discussion about the differences, but here we are simply looking at the idea of police and correctional officer subculture in general terms, and how its constraints may influence the individual officer's sense of autonomy in the workplace.

What, then, are some of the distinguishing characteristics of police and correctional officer subculture, and why is it sometimes claimed that this subculture is different from that in most other workplaces?

Support for seeing the two subcultures as similar is offered by Elizabeth Grossi and Bruce Berg (1991), to whom we referred earlier. They write:

"Those who have studied the internal workings of correctional institutions may recognize that powerful forces within the correctional system have a stronger influence over the behaviour of correctional officers than the administrators of the institution, legislative decrees, or agency policies. These social forces may be understood as related to a 'correctional officer subculture,' similar to that found in policing." (p. 79)

These two writers list what they call "setting-related stressors" for correctional officers that they claim are "remarkably similar to those commonly associated with police officers." (p. 79)

1. The ever-present potential for physical danger.
2. Hostility directed at officers by inmates, their [inmate] families and often even the public.
3. Unreasonable demands and expectations on their role as correctional officers; vacillating political attitudes toward the institutional role of corrections.
4. A tedious and unrewarding work environment.
5. The dependence correctional officers place on one another to effectively work in the institution safely.
6. The reality that one cannot always expect to act the way either one would choose to, or the way the public might expect them to.

(Point 6 is one of the few references I have found to support the idea that police and correctional officer subculture may impair the ability of the individual officer to make independent moral and practical decisions at work.)

Kelsey Kauffman (1988) is a scholar who researches primarily in the corrections context. In her book entitled *Prison Officers and Their World*, based on a four-year study of the Massachusetts prison system, she says, "Officers also possess a distinct subculture within prisons. Their own beliefs and code of conduct set them apart from administrators, social workers, and, of course, inmates." She "discovered" the beliefs and the norms that constitute the code of conduct by asking officers two questions: a) What is the worst thing you could do in your own eyes as an officer?, and b) What is the worst thing you could do in the eyes of other officers? Nine norms were identified:

1. Always go to the aid of an officer in distress.
2. Do not "lug" drugs.
3. Do not "rat."

4. Never make a fellow officer look bad in front of inmates.

5. Always support an officer in a dispute with an inmate.

6. Always support officer sanctions against inmates.

7. Do not be a "white hat." (This denotes any behaviour suggesting sympathy for or identification with inmates.)

8. Maintain officer solidarity against all outside groups.

9. Show positive concern for fellow officers. (p. 85)

Would it be reasonable to suggest that if we substituted the word "criminal," "offender" or "suspect" for "inmate," many of these norms would apply equally to policing? Clearly, the predominant theme here is that of *solidarity* of the officers, and of support and protection of one another in the face of the common "enemy." The enemy is the criminal element and, to a lesser extent, outside groups and the public.

Let me offer an illustration of this point about officer solidarity. A newspaper article entitled "Four officers suspended in probe" indicated that four police officers had been suspended pending a probe into allegations that they had planted drugs on suspects (*The Toronto Star*, March 17, 1995, p. A6). The article included the comment: "Detectives from the force's internal affairs unit launched their probe two weeks ago after a constable—whose identity is a closely guarded secret—complained that a veteran officer from 12 Division's B Platoon had been involved in illegal conduct....Meanwhile, the name and division of the police officer who made the complaint are being kept secret. Police sources say they don't know what motivated the constable to come forward with the allegations at this time."

It would be inappropriate to read too much into this newspaper account. However, on the face of it we may have an example of one police officer feeling the need to "break ranks" and report behaviour of colleagues that he considered unacceptable or even illegal. That the reporting officer's identity was kept a "closely guarded secret" should come as little or no surprise because of the potential for being ostracised by the group. (As an aside, there is a conundrum here for the administrator to whom the officer reported the wrongdoing. The administrator has to weigh keeping the confidence of the reporting officer against the right of his or her accused colleagues to know who the accuser is. We shall return to difficulties like this one later when we discuss the ethical dilemmas). If Kelsey Kauffman is correct, this reporting officer failed to comply with at least eight of the nine subcultural norms. Please look at the norms and identify for yourself how many you think were breached by the officer. He is guilty of "breaking ranks," of not remaining "solid" with the officer group.

You are correct if you are thinking we haven't yet identified what makes a subculture in the justice context substantively different from that in other workplaces. One writer, Vernon Fox (1983), talks about one difference in his book *Correctional Institutions*. He notes that much has been written about the loyalty of police to their colleagues and affirms that such loyalties are also common in the corporate world. "Nevertheless," he says, "this loyalty appears to be stronger and have more meaning in the criminal justice system than in most other groups." (p. 162) Some of you might disagree with Fox. You may argue that the subculture in General Motors, for example, is similar in many respects. You may well be correct.

One important difference, however, is the anti-criminal element. Most other workplaces see the customers in positive terms, often as "friends." If they did not, they would probably not survive for very long! Offenders, on the other hand—the "clients" of police and correctional officers—excite a different response, normally one characterized by antipathy. And this antipathy can create a bond among police and correctional officers as they see themselves working together against the "bad guys."

One other even more significant factor may account for the difference between subculture in corrections and policing, and that in other workplaces. In policing and corrections there is an ever-present potential for danger—life-threatening danger. The potential for danger exists because of who the "clients" are. There are significant issues around personal safety that generally do not characterize most other workplaces. And it is this ingredient of danger that may lend credibility to the view that police and correctional officer subculture is stronger.

If the subculture is stronger, it may be reasonable to think of it as a more compelling constraint on the conduct of its members.

Some interesting work was done in the 1960s on group solidarity by sociologist Irving Janis. Janis, basing much of his theorizing on war incidents, supported the idea that the presence of danger tends to increase the solidarity of a group. For example, he said: "It has long been known that when people are exposed to external danger they show a remarkable increase in group solidarity. That is, they manifest increased motivation to retain affiliation with a face-to-face group and to avoid actions that deviate from its norms. (p. 80)

This, I believe, is the key difference between police and correctional officer subculture, and subculture in most other workplaces. The individual officer's welfare, if not her life, can sometimes rest in the hands of a partner. The willingness of colleagues to respond, support and provide "backup" in an emergency, is a basic tenet of the police and correctional officer's role. This, I would suggest, can in turn lead to a bonding that goes beyond the kind one might expect in most other workplaces.

Security issues and the way in which individual officers have to rely on each other for their safety makes the requirement to remain loyal to one another the key norm in their subculture. There is a strong prohibition against what is often called "ratting" or "ratting out" of a colleague. Coincidental with writing this section of the book, I was conducting a seminar at a secure, young-offender facility. The officers and I engaged in a conversation about this topic. At the end of the day one of the staff came up to me, and surreptitiously pulled from his pocket his electronic key fob, on one side of which he had placed a picture of a rat. He had reported a colleague for hitting a resident, had been labelled a rat, and had decorated his key fob in this way as a humorous attempt to neutralize the stress of his "label." It is not unknown in corrections or policing for rather severe consequences to be inflicted upon a colleague who has been labelled a "rat" by his colleagues. These consequences can range from being "put on the grease" (shunned by colleagues) to threats of personal or property harm being made—or carried out—against the "rat."

The television news program *60 Minutes* carried a story that may be pertinent to this discussion. According to the story, aired at the time this chapter was being written (CBS News, March 30, 1997), two officers named Rigg and Caruso at California's Corcoran State Penitentiary blew the whistle on what they considered to be unethical conduct by their colleagues. The two officers claim that inmates from different ethnic groups were set up to fight gladiator-style in the small exercise yard of the Special Handling Unit. It was not unusual, they claimed, for officers to place bets on the outcome of the fights. When the fights got out of hand, they claimed, officers would on occasion shoot at the inmates. Since the institution had opened in 1988, eight inmates had been shot dead by officers and numerous others had been wounded. Inmate Preston Tate, it was claimed, was told after he had hit an officer that he would never get out of the facility alive. On the program, videotape footage was shown of Tate and another inmate of the same ethnic origin fighting two other inmates of a different origin. Tate was shot and killed in the melee even though the videotape clearly shows that he was not the aggressor and that he was away from the fight when he was shot. Lieutenant Rigg, one of the whistle-blowing officers, described the shooting of the inmate as murder.

Whether the allegations are true has not yet been determined and is immaterial to the point I am about to make. During the interview with the two officers, both said they had been labelled as "rats," as "no-goods," and both had had their lives threatened by officer colleagues. Even though they had been transferred to other institutions the labels travelled with them, which made their lives in their new workplaces as miserable as they had been at Corcoran. At the conclusion of the story, interviewer Mike Wallace, at the new place of work of officer Richard Caruso, hailed down the vehicle doing the institution perimeter check and asked the officer driving the vehicle if he would shake hands with Caruso. It was a telling moment when the driver looked incredulously at Wallace, shook his head in a gesture of defiance, and drove off. Breaking ranks and being labelled a rat can be an unpleasant, unsettling experience.

In the mid-1980s, a female correctional officer at a medium security correctional institution reported some of her colleagues for sleeping on night shift. She had reportedly approached them and said several times that she felt unsafe and vulnerable when they were asleep. She told them that if they did not refrain from doing so, she would have no alternative but to report them to the superintendent. They continued. She reported them. The consequences for her were severe. Graffiti was written about her on some of the walls in the institution; she received harassing phone calls and letters; her car was deliberately damaged in the institution parking lot. The campaign of terror by her colleagues culminated in some bricks thrown through the windows of her home. It appears she paid a heavy price for doing what she considered to be the right thing. In this case, the right thing for her was to attempt to ensure her own safety and that of the institution.

It was many years ago now, but I remember experiencing a three-week ride-along with a police force. In a ride-along program, as many of you will know, a civilian is taken along in a cruiser to observe police officers at work. I had been invited to do so after spending several weeks conducting in-service training sessions for this particular police force. I had also got to know several officers through a Criminology course I was teaching at a local community college. The officers had accepted me and became very open with me about their work, about their rites of passage and about what they considered the "perks" of their job. I remember riding along with one particular officer who appeared not to be well-liked or well-respected by his colleagues. I noticed that the other officers were invariably slower to respond to his calls for assistance. I questioned them about this apparent antipathy because I could not make any sense of their reaction to this officer. He struck me as being a professional, principled, family-oriented individual. In retrospect I can see that he was deemed by his colleagues not to fit in. Several years later, I think that I can see why they may have reacted to him in this way. He was not one of "them." He marched to his own drummer.

He refused to participate in the on-duty activities of some his colleagues, some of which, I remember, stretched the limits of professional conduct.

This will probably not come as any great surprise to you, but I think it is interesting that the inmate subculture is also characterized by what we will call the loyalty norm. Anyone who has worked in the justice field, particularly those of you who have worked in correctional institutions, will be familiar with the way in which inmates are quick and sometimes merciless in weeding out from their number those they consider to be "rats." This is one of the main reasons most institutions have protective custody or super-protective custody wings, ranges or cell blocks—so that inmate "rats" can be segregated for their own protection.

Perhaps you will permit me to make a personal observation. In my ethics seminars I discuss the issue of subculture and the police or correctional officer participants are generally quick to identify the "ratting" norm as a key one. In addition to the term "rat," they use, almost interchangeably, terms like "narc" or "fink." In Australia, the act of reporting a colleague is often called "dobbing in a mate"—a sin in the Australian culture considered almost equivalent to blasphemy! (It would be interesting for someone to investigate whether or not this strong societal norm resides in Australia's history of being settled by convicts.) In the seminars, the participants, when asked about the effects of the "ratting" norm on their individual sense of what may or may not be the right thing to do, become deeply reflective. And this happens almost without exception. It is as though the participants are taking personal stock of where they are as individuals with respect to this issue. When I question them about the apparent change of "chemistry" in the room, they generally confirm that this is precisely what is happening—that they are engaging in a personal check regarding how much of their individuality they may have conceded to their colleague group.

A Need for a Sense of Perspective

It would be wrong to discuss this issue of officer subculture and to fail to point out that the subculture has some extremely positive qualities. The mutual support and protection it is likely to engender in crisis situations is essential to the well-being of the officers. The camaraderie often experienced following a crisis situation is sometimes essential to the emotional and psychological health of officers involved. The feeling of belonging to a group whose members understand the peculiar and difficult demands of the profession can be a gratifying and comforting experience, especially when the group or the profession feels under siege from the public.

This camaraderie and support that police officers have with and for each other is graphically expressed in an article entitled "Courtroom 'tense' for detective in shooting" (*The Toronto Star*, March 7, 1997, p. A6). A detective, charged after a teen was shot in the head and killed, was supported by "more than 100 off-duty York Region officers."

One justice educator I was speaking with talked about this positive side. "The subculture at times can be a strength. At times, you may be asked as an officer to do some fairly disgusting things....Once the incident is over, you still have your 'family' to support you." Continuing this thought, another officer said, "The subculture serves you well. There is a lot of camaraderie. I think people do look after each other. There is a recognition coming from one's peers that is more valued than that coming from administrators."

It would be inappropriate to expect individuals involved in the dangerous professions of policing and corrections to "go it alone." Indeed it would be, and is, a distinct worry for both colleagues and managers to have to work with a maverick, "loner" officer.

This chapter and the next are not about breaking the subculture. They simply raise the question as to whether, on occasion, the officer subculture can have a darker side; a side where too much of a person's sense of independence and individuality is given up to the group, even when the group may be acting against the moral suasion of that individual. Remember, in Chapter 1 we called it de-individuation.

Summary

To summarize, in this section of the chapter we have discussed whether there are sufficient similarities between subcultures in policing and corrections to allow us to consider them, for the purposes of this book, as essentially similar. It was suggested that an argument could be made for doing so, although the finer differences between them would make for an interesting research topic.

By way of explaining the similarities between the two subcultures, certain norms, probably common to both, were identified.

The essential similarities are created and reinforced, we suggested, first, by the inherent danger in both roles—there are distinct and ever-present risks to the safety and well-being of the officers; second, by the reality that in these two subcultures the general feeling toward the "client" is one of antipathy, a situation not generally found in other workplaces in government, industry or commerce; third, by a shared antipathy toward the public "them" who do not understand "us."

Because of these factors we have suggested that policing and corrections subcultures are, in some significant ways, different from "regular" workplace subcultures, and that the most significant difference—the threat to the officers' safety—ensures to a greater degree than in other workplaces that the loyalty norm is respected by individuals and enforced by the group.

Reflections

What are your views about whether police officer and correctional officer subcultures are generally similar?

What are your views about the idea that there are some significant differences between police and correctional officer subculture, and subcultures in most other workplaces?

What do you think of the nine correctional officer subcultural norms identified by Kelsey Kauffman and the six stressors identified by Elizabeth Grossi and Bruce Berg? Which ones, if any, do you think would apply to police officers?

5

Subculture: What the Practitioners Think

I know what the officer code is and it is very strong. A person can come into this work with all good intentions, but a lot of people just give up and fall into the pit [the subculture].
— *Senior federal institution administrator.*

After reading this chapter, you should be able to

- Explain why it may be risky for a police or correctional officer to talk openly about the group norms that govern his conduct
- Identify three key ideas that practitioners have about officer subculture and subcultural constraints
- Explain why subcultural constraints may make it difficult for officers to make autonomous moral decisions at work
- Explain the terms **loyalty** and **solidarity** in the context of a justice subculture
- Explain why there may be a link between officer and offender subculture
- Identify one reason why some officers may be able to take moral stands on certain issues and not be ostracised by their colleagues
- Explain why members of a subculture need to identify common "enemies," and what effect this has on the group

A Sensitive Topic

Much of the material for this chapter has been gathered in one-on-one personal interviews. The interviews were conducted with justice educators, police and correctional officers, and correctional institution and police administrators. The transcripts of many of the interviews constitute a part of the qualitative data gathered for my doctoral dissertation. The material is included here with the written consent of the respondents. Great care has been taken not to identify any police force, correctional jurisdiction or institution, or individual officer. The willingness of these people to speak to me is much appreciated. They have contributed significantly to my learning, and I hope their insights will contribute to your learning also.

The issue of subculture in policing and corrections is a highly sensitive and emotive one. In their willingness to express their views on this topic, some of these individuals, particularly officers, took extraordinary risks. The nature of these risks may become more apparent as the chapter unfolds.

To illustrate the risk-taking, let me recount part of a conversation I had with one officer. As we were concluding the interview I asked the officer if he had any last thoughts about our discussion. The officer confided: "It is difficult. I have found this a difficult interview. I'm finding it (the subculture) is something that you don't talk with everybody about, and it is just, I don't know it's...." "It's a question of trust," I finished, "and you don't know me from a hole in the ground." "That's it right there," the officer replied, "I think, too, because I am at work I have this shield up around me to protect me....The co-workers are the only ones you can really trust."

Another officer, in response to my invitation to make some final comments on our discussion, said: "This had better not get out or I'm in deep doo-doo."

It should be pointed out that the officers interviewed were selected randomly; it was not the case, by way of allaying any suspicion you may have about the process, that these officers were handpicked in some way. When you read some of their comments, you may be tempted to think they were selected for interview because they had been identified as loose cannons or had already been targets for ostracism by their colleagues. This was not the case, either. Before interviewing them I had little or no idea of what their perspectives were going to be, or what risks they would take in sharing their ideas with me.

This chapter is organized around the various points of discussion in the preceding chapter. We continue to explore the terms "subculture" and "subcultural constraints." We discuss in greater depth whether police and correctional officer subculture is different from subculture in other workplaces. We continue to explore the links between officer subculture and criminal subculture. We also look at the idea that the subculture is stronger in the justice context and that, as a result, the norms are more compelling on individual officers.

It should, of course, be kept in mind that this discussion does not constitute the definitive word on any point discussed. It is included here simply as a means of fleshing out the discussion in Chapter 4. By including and thinking about some of the ideas of police and correctional practitioners, we may be able to develop a broader understanding of the issue. In this chapter, their perspectives have been interlaced with researcher ideas and with some case studies, by way of providing a context for these perspectives. Hopefully, the discussion will serve the purpose of providing further background for your thinking and debating.

"Subculture" and "Subcultural Constraints"

Throughout the interviews with the educator, officer and administrator groups, certain terms kept recurring:

bonding	adherence
code of silence	code of behaviour
officer code	what officers have to do
unwritten code	conformity
sticking together	non-conformity
loss of individuality	loyalty
put on the grease	ratting
family	social control
ostracised	peer pressure

These terms are referred to consistently. They are, I would suggest, key to our understanding of subculture in the justice context. We should acknowledge, of course, that they can also be key to subcultures in other workplaces. What we have to keep in mind is the *degree* to which these terms characterize a particular subculture. As I have suggested, and this is borne out by the discussion that follows, they apply to a high degree in police and correctional officer subculture, especially when we consider maximum security institutions. They would also apply, to a lesser degree, in medium and minimum security facilities.

What did the individuals I interviewed have to say in general about subculture and subcultural constraints?

The officer subculture was defined in various ways. One respondent, for example, talked about the subculture as an unwritten but organized set of values that are communicated among the staff. Others talked about the code as an informal one, but one which, nonetheless, is known by all officers. Despite its informality, and despite the fact that it is unwritten, the code is often thought of as having a strong influence on the behaviour of officers. One experienced administrator, who had himself come up through the ranks, described the subculture as a force that has the potential to make a "major impact on the judgment of officers."

The loyalty or solidarity issue seemed to loom large in many of the responses. One justice educator, in describing subculture in the corrections context, said, "It seems to me that what you get is that same 'protect your own self and your partners' mentality that I see in other areas of law enforcement…where regardless of how serious the violation of either a code of ethics or a violation of policy, people have convinced themselves it is wrong to 'rat.'" Another educator talked in terms of there existing a very strong expectation to remain "solid." Some people talked about the loyalty or solidarity requirement as though it were part of the unwritten code. "I believe," said one person, "there's a code among officers—you don't put it on a fellow officer. If you go outside the norm and inform, I think you'll have a great deal of difficulty." Another said, "The downside is that there is a tremendous amount of pressure to conform with one's peers in ways that could put one at great, I'd say ethical, and sometimes even in legal jeopardy."

What is this pressure, and what might be the consequences of resisting it?

One educator, a former officer, said that "if you choose as an officer not to conform, you would be brought under a significant amount of social control within a very, very brief period of time. I have situations where people have had to deal with crisis situations on their own because they are now perceived as a loner, and as somebody the rest of the officers don't want to have anything to do with, because they are not conforming."

The officers invariably confirmed this idea that there would be considerable risk of social isolation for a colleague labelled as a "rat." "If you rat on somebody, you tend to lose a lot of friends, and, basically, you are left with no-one to turn to for anything," said one. Another officer said, "You wouldn't want to 'rat out' on a fellow officer. It is something you just wouldn't do. You would be labelled a 'rat.'" I asked another person what the consequences might be, if any, for any officer reporting a serious infraction of a colleague. "I believe I would be shunned. I would be given a hard time. I would be an outcast. I would be labelled a rat." This shunning, as this officer put it, was often referred to in the interviews as "being put on the grease." For example, one officer said, "You put them on the grease. You don't talk to them, you don't sit with them. You treat them like outcasts."

The rule of thumb—the basic expectation—said another officer, was that "you keep your mouth shut and do not rat other people out." He indicated that the rule was that "if you saw a colleague doing something wrong, that was his/her business." As a brief aside here, one of the more disturbing aspects of working with justice students prior to, and after completion of, their field practicum is that one sees a value shift in individual students from an "I don't think I could let that go" (about a serious officer indiscretion) attitude prior to placement to a "so long as I don't do it—what she does is her business" attitude afterwards.

A trainee police officer recounted to me some advice given to him during his first few days at a police detachment: "The first day I was there, you know, after having met me and that type of thing, they [the officers] took me in their office and basically had a chat with me. They said whatever you see here, you keep your mouth shut you don't say nothing [sic]. I kind of looked at that two ways. You know, you see a lot of stuff the general public shouldn't be told about, but also maybe there was a kind of double meaning there. Maybe they were also telling me, whatever you and the other cops are up to out there, don't be going and squealing to his boss or something."

One correctional officer in a maximum security institution went so far as to say that it would be virtually impossible for someone declared to be a rat to survive in that facility. He also indicated that it would be equally unlikely that such an officer would survive in another institution because the officer grapevine, much like the inmate grapevine, would send word to that institution that this staff member was not to be trusted. Of an officer declared to be a rat, he said: "There is no way you can last more than a month or two months with the type of abuse you would take in this institution." He said the abuse would probably take the form of the "rat" being treated with "dead silence," having letters mailed to him with "rat" on the address, having her tires slashed, or "whatever." When asked to elaborate on what "whatever" may have signified, the officer declined to do so.

To draw this section of the chapter to a close, another officer was direct about what expectations the officers have of each other. "Say a situation happened and something didn't go down the way it was supposed to, and an officer is in the wrong. You don't bring this to anyone's attention, you stick together as a unit and you write reports as a unit." An administrator said something similar: "It is not unusual to have people sit down collectively and write reports. The individual who deviates away from his peers runs the risk of ostracisation. They run the risk of outright intimidation from time to time."

What can also happen—and this is a fairly common theme in the interviews—is that if you see a wrongdoing by a colleague and you are questioned about it, you will simply respond that you did not see anything. What is implied here is that there may be times when individual officers are required to write reports or respond in a way they know to be patently false. They know that what they are writing is essentially a lie and they may feel bad about it, but the expectation is for them to become part of an event that is unethical and/or illegal—or face the consequences.

If you think about it, these are difficult circumstances under which to make personal, individual moral decisions.

I don't say this by way of judging you or your colleagues. I feel for you as you wrestle with the fine tension between the basic human (and professional) need you have to be accepted by your colleague group, and the need for you to be able to do what you consider to be the right thing in a given situation. I know your struggle. I have been there. I don't set myself up here as a paragon of virtue, or as someone having a monopoly on wisdom. I raise the issue of subcultural constraints and individual moral decision-making because I think it should be raised, as difficult as it is to do so. But I raise the issue in a spirit of compassion, not of judgment.

It is important at this juncture that we add some riders. It would be wrong for anyone to suggest that there are no individual officers who have managed to achieve a status with their colleagues such that they can take their own moral stands and survive in their groups. Generally, these are officers who are experienced and respected as professionals; they are people who have proven themselves in dangerous situations and are seen as colleagues who can be counted upon in a crisis. On occasion these individuals can, and do, take risks with their group that younger officers dare not take.

It would also be wrong not to add that there are sometimes significant individual differences even among the younger officers. Some are stronger than others, and are able to take more courageous stands, despite the subcultural pressures against doing so.

Another interesting idea that came out of my research—and this has been confirmed in several conversations since—is that there may be a gender difference with respect to the personal stands that officers are prepared to take. I hear that women are more likely to take stands. I also hear that this may be due to the fact that they are not subject to the potential for "parking lot justice" that males may sometimes expect. It would be quite inappropriate, of course, to place too much stock in this idea at this time. And we should beware of making gross generalizations based on some personal observations. The idea of gender difference and moral courage may, however, be an interesting topic for further exploration in your classes.

One final note. In some of the conversations I have had with officers and administrators, reference has been made to the idea that an ostracised officer could not be sure of backup in an emergency. It needs to be pointed out—and this, too, has been confirmed for me in less formal conversations with various individuals—that even someone who has been declared a "rat" will almost invariably be afforded colleague support in a crisis situation.

What do you think of the comments of your fellow officers included in this section of the chapter? If you agree with all or some of them, would you be prepared to express them to

a. a researcher you did not know?

b. your colleagues?

c. your manager?

d. your teacher?

A number of key terms relating to officer subculture are listed. Which ones, if any, would you agree are significant in developing a better understanding of the norms governing your colleague group?

Why is it, do you think, that an unwritten, informal code of conduct can potentially have such a powerful influence over the decision-making and behaviour of individual officers?

One officer said: "There is a tremendous amount of pressure to conform with one's peers in ways that could put one at great ethical, and sometimes even legal jeopardy." How would you respond to this statement?

Should there be a place for discussion of officer subculture in your training or education? If so, why? If not, why not?

In your view or experience, are female officers more or less likely than males to take a stand on moral issues that relate to corrections or policing?

Let us now look at what some of your colleagues and managers have to say about the potential links between the subculture of officers and that of their "clients."

Links Between Officer Subculture and Criminal Subculture

This section applies principally to correctional officers, but there are pieces that may apply to police officers. In the case of correctional officers, of course, we are talking about imprisoned offenders, and in the case of police officers we would be thinking more of the "street" criminal subculture.

It's a troubling idea, I suppose, that there may be some similarities between the subcultural norms that govern the conduct of those in the criminal world and those that can sometimes govern the conduct of officers. But the links appear to be there, nonetheless. This was a common theme in the interviews I conducted. Consider how Vernon Fox (1983) in *Correctional Institutions* describes prisoner subculture, and think about whether there may be some parallels with the way police and correctional officers govern each other's conduct at work: "The inmate code in a maximum security prison is made up of the customs and folkways by which the residents protect themselves from the repressive measures of the administration; the inmates have nothing to do with the administration or correctional officers, and they do not 'squeal' or 'snitch' on fellow inmates. This inmate code, which is fundamental to prison organization, manifests itself in a type of informal control...." (p. 101)

Perhaps it is not surprising, then, that one correctional officer I interviewed said that in his view, the officer subculture is defined by the subculture of what he called the "clients we serve." The officer said: "So a lot of the subculture that you would see among correctional officers is very defined by the inmate subculture." He added: "One doesn't have to work long in institutions to find that people take on the manners of the inmates and their culture."

You will know, whether you are a police officer or a correctional officer, or a student or trainee preparing for either one of these professions, that there is a strong code of conduct that governs the behaviour of the criminal element on the street, as it does the conduct of inmates in institutions. As we noted earlier, any criminal person not considered "solid"—where "solid" means, in essence, fully committed to the group and its code of conduct, including a code of silence—lives dangerously. In an institution, an individual identified as not "solid" often needs to be separated for his own protection. On the street, police informers live equally dangerously. I think it is clear that this value of absolute loyalty to the group can and often does govern officer conduct.

Where this de-individuating value has its roots is a moot point. I call it a de-individuating value because it requires the individual to sacrifice individuality in the interests of the collective. Did this value start with the officers, such that the criminal element adopted the value for itself for its own protection, or was it the other way around? One person I interviewed saw it this way: "I think there is a correctional officer subculture that originates or takes its origins from the inmate subculture. I think it is just as devious and I think it has as much of a dark side as the inmate subculture." Another person said: "So I think it is a learned form of behaviour [the requirement not to 'rat'] that isn't attributed in the system to the inmates, but in my estimation that is where the staff pick it up. They start to play a similar role in how they interact with each other to the way the inmates do."

Wherever the answer concerning the origin of the loyalty norm, one thing seems clear. If you have that sense of solidarity on one side of the fence, you are probably going to have it on the other side. It is, after all, a very human way to react. It probably has something to do with presenting a united, mutually protecting front against a common "enemy." One correctional officer expressed this idea well when he said: "I think the inmate code influences us in the fact that you have two distinct groups. You have got the inmates and they will do whatever they can to get by you, and they will stick together no matter what. And we have the same idea; if we are going to have any luck in controlling this place we are going to have to stick together too."

If what we have discussed so far is at least part of the dynamic constituting criminal and officer subculture, then we can see how the breaking of ranks by a member of either the officer or offender group is not going to elicit a positive response from that member's group.

So what did the practitioners who were interviewed have to say about all this? Not surprisingly, they offered some interesting and, I would have to say, sobering ideas. We don't like to think of ourselves as sharing *any* values with offenders, do we? But in fact we probably do.

By way of introducing their ideas, Mark Baker (1985), in his book *Cops: Their Lives in Their Own Words,* quotes a police officer as saying: "The mentality [of police officers] is an organized crime mentality. It is to be respected in some ways, but it has to be respected from the perspective of criminality, not from legitimate law enforcement. The culture that we come from and the kind of country that we live in, we do respect that kind of camaraderie. But it's magnified in police work. It can go too far." (p. 175)

May I suggest that Baker, even though he does not elaborate on the point, is suggesting by the phrase "It can go too far" that carrying the norms of loyalty and solidarity in police work too far can and sometimes does result in unethical conduct on the part of some individual officers. This sometimes blind allegiance to the loyalty norm can create fertile ground for officer behaviour ranging from poor judgment at one end of the spectrum to corruption at the other end.

A graphic example took place in Toronto. Two Metropolitan Toronto police officers were charged with planting drugs on a suspect whom they subsequently charged with possession. In their trial, evidence was given by a young, 26-year-old police officer, who had been convicted (and dismissed from the force) earlier for attempting to obstruct justice in the case by falsifying his notebook entries.

In a newspaper account of the court proceedings, the young officer offered the following in his defence: "I went along with the flow. I went ahead with it....I didn't want to rock the boat." He said he was very uncomfortable with his actions but continued in this way to justify them: "I wouldn't have much of a career left as far as people working with me....You're supposed to be a team player." (*The Globe and Mail*, October 23, 1996, p. A9)

Maureen Prinsloo, chair of the Metropolitan Toronto Police Board, made a decision to tour some police stations after the two accused officers in the above case were found not guilty of planting drugs on the suspect. In a newspaper account of her visits, Prinsloo is quoted as saying "the vast majority of officers simply did their jobs." The article continues: "However, she said, when she asked 'Why do you turn a blind eye to this small group who will pull your reputation down?' I got no answer." "To Serve and Protect (the force's motto)," she said, "that is to serve and protect the public. It does not mean protecting the bad ones in your midst." (*The Toronto Star*, November 21, 1996, p. A6)

One justice educator, an experienced correctional practitioner, indicated what he considers to be the cardinal norm in both subcultures. He said, "an inmate doesn't inform on an inmate, and an officer doesn't inform on an officer." And another officer said: "Just like the inmates have an unwritten rule that they don't rat out on each other, so it's an unwritten rule that officers don't rat out on each other....Our code and theirs is basically the same code."

Another educator, a former officer and administrator, took this theme further. "But I also think of the unethical practices with respect to the subculture. I think the prisoner subculture has rules like 'you don't rat'....Well, a similar process happens for correctional officers where they will be under pressure not to say anything if one of their co-workers does something that is considered to be against the rules. For example, hits an inmate, beats an inmate up, steals from an inmate, misrepresents the facts in a report....New staff may be pressured to learn very quickly an opposite way of doing things from the way in which they have been taught. You join the system. But you get that way, you pick it up—in the same way police officers do."

It's pertinent that a connection is being made between the subcultural pressures one can feel as an officer and what this person calls "unethical practices." It is critically important that we refrain from making any overgeneralized or *carte blanche* statements about the possibility of this connection, but it is a question that deserves serious and open-minded attention.

Some of the officers interviewed talked about other shared values between the officer and inmate subcultures. One institution administrator, for example, talked about how both the inmates and the officers see the sex offender as on the lowest rung of the ladder in the inmate hierarchy.

Others talked about the way language is shared by the two subcultures. One officer said of his colleagues: "I think they pick it [the language] up from the inmate subculture. It is a strange thing but they pick up the inmate jargon. They talk about 'don't crack to me,' an inmate expression which means don't talk to me. Both groups use expressions like 'put on the dummy,' 'cheese eaters,' 'laying track,' that kind of thing." Those who have worked in the justice system will also be aware of expressions like "bit" (sentence), "diddlers" (child molesters), "'deuce less" (two years less a day), "six" (officer coming), "the hole" (segregation), or "queen" (effeminate male inmate who may or may not be in the process of a sex change), to name just a few terms often used interchangeably by prisoners and officers. Many of these terms, of course, apply principally in the context of correctional institutions.

Police officers also share a common language with the criminal subculture. They, like correctional officers, would use terms like "rat," "fink" or "narc," and "diddlers." In the United States, police officers talk about "stand-up guys" (officers who will protect a colleague who has done something wrong), and "hand-up guys" (officers who will do the opposite). The terms refer, essentially, to officers who are considered solid or not solid. Police officers may also use terms like "screw" (correctional officer), "joint" (jail), "hopped up" (under the influence of drugs), "roach" (the butt of a marijuana cigarette), and "score" (to purchase drugs). Mark Baker (1985) in *Cops* quotes one police officer as telling him: "So many police terms are picked up from the street world and become incorporated in police mentality [and language]." (p. 199)

Who influences whom in the use of this common argot? I put this question to an institution administrator who stated very clearly his view that it was the inmate language that influenced the language of the officers. He said: "You don't have inmates going around talking like correctional officers or acting like them in any way, shape, or form."

Reflections

Would you agree there may be some links between officer subculture and criminal subculture?

If you agree, what would some of these links be? Can you think of some of your own?

Do you agree that officers and the criminal group can come to share a jargon?

Subculture and "Enemies"

We have suggested that subcultures are stronger and may require for their existence an identifiable common enemy. In the case of police and correctional officer subculture we have suggested that the "enemy" may take three forms. First, the criminal element; second, the administration; and, third, the public.

It should be pointed out that the primary target for officers' antipathy is the offender group, followed in order by the administration, and the public. This is summed up nicely by Mark Baker (1985), also in *Cops*, talks about police officers' attitudes toward these groups. "Many cops begin to see themselves as under siege from all sides. They develop a classic 'Us versus Them' mentality....The real reason most police officers socialize exclusively with other police officers is that they just don't trust the people they police—which is everybody who is not a cop....Older officers teach younger ones that it is best to avoid civilians....The 'Us against Them' attitude also applies within the ranks of the police themselves. Superior officers from sergeants on up are regarded by patrol officers as 'Them.'" (pp. 175-176)

Anti-criminal

It should be acknowledged that there are two scholars who, in the context of corrections, argue that correctional officers are not as anti-inmate in their disposition as they themselves, and others, sometimes think they are. John Klofas and Hans Toch (1982) developed the concept of "pluralistic ignorance" among correctional officers. Based on a survey of correctional officers, they are of the opinion that there are what they call "progressive" officers (officers who are not anti-inmate) who, thinking they are in the minority, are, in fact, in the majority. Likewise, officers with non-progressive (anti-inmate) views, feeling themselves to be in the majority, are, in fact, in the minority.

The results and conclusions of their survey are curious. My research and experience present a different picture—that officers in the main are, or become, anti-inmate in disposition. One or two experiences of being "conned" or manipulated by an inmate can quickly change the positive officer into a suspicious one who sees the inmate group as the enemy. And generally speaking, any officer who continues to be essentially pro-inmate in the face of such experiences is often viewed with great suspicion by his officer colleagues.

One administrator I interviewed said: "I know what the code is and it is very strong. A person [new officer] can come into this work with all good intentions, but a lot of people just give up and fall into the anti-inmate routine because it is easier—make your money, go home, and forget about it." And another officer talked about how an officer's attitude towards inmates can change: "It's a funny thing. When you first start here, you tend to sympathize and empathize with the inmates, but after dealing with them on a daily basis, when you are treated badly, in a way you are almost happy if something does happen to them."

One officer made a stronger statement when he talked about officers having "an inherent dislike for inmates, not a feeling of revulsion necessarily, but certainly a dislike for most of the inmate population just simply because they are inmates."

In the case of police officers, the case is an even clearer-cut one. There is a strong antipathy towards those who break the law, and who represent, potentially, personal danger for the officer. In a chapter of *Cops* entitled "Blood Brothers," Baker (1985) talks about how this antipathy towards lawbreakers and the danger they represent can galvanize police officers into a solid group. "Nobody understands but another cop," one officer is quoted as saying.

Let's take a brief look at what people in my interviews had to say about these antipathies.

One clinical psychologist who works in the justice field talked about how the relationship between officer and offender is characterized by an "us" against "them" attitude, and he attributed the binding together of both officer and inmate groups to this way of thinking and feeling. An experienced administrator and former officer had this to say about institution subculture: "It is 'them' against 'us', 'them' being the inmates or the administration, depending on the issue." An officer expressed some strong anti-inmate sentiments: "You are dealing with people who go against every principle you have in your life. You are on the other side....You have got them treating you like you are a lowlife." Another officer was even more strident in his account: "The minute you walk through the door, you are in a whole different environment....If the inmates can get something off you they will lie through their teeth to get it....You get burned a couple of times by inmates and, yeah, you are going to come out with a very cynical attitude—and that is the attitude you have in this place." One female officer, equally strident, said: "The general public has no idea what kind of animals society has locked up, and you are dealing with these people on a daily basis....You are no longer part of a polite society now you are in amongst animals...."

Police officers express similar sentiments about their professional lives and the kind of people they have to encounter during the course of their duties.

Anti-administration

The anti-administration feelings police and correctional officers can develop is illustrated by an event that took place in the Metropolitan Toronto police force in January 1995. A one-day illegal strike of police officers took place in 51 Division. The deputy police chief had decided to order a public inquiry into the conduct of two officers from that Division, and this decision precipitated the strike. One of the columnists in *The Toronto Star* (January 30, 1995, p. A6) wrote this about the incident: "When you try to penetrate the miasma of cop culture, this is what happens. When you cross the line of blind allegiance to cop fraternity, this is what occurs. Politicians are given an ultimatum. The public is threatened with the withdrawal of vital services. And the full ferocity of cop wrath descends on the head of the deputy chief who was already seen—because of his commitment to accountability and procedural reform—as the enemy."

A correctional officer summed up this anti-administration idea succinctly when she said: "Because the management is after us, you cannot have everybody running around totally against each other." And another officer resorted to the use of inmate jargon to explain where he stood on this issue: "You don't talk to them [the management], you don't 'crack' to them, only in the line of business. You just say the minimal amount that you have to say to them to get the job done."

Anti-public

Finally, here are two sentiments, one expressed by a corrections educator, the other by a police educator who had worked as a police officer for many years. The former talked about what he called the "hunker down" mentality of officers. To explain what he meant by hunker down, he talked about "inmate against guard, guard against inmate, guard against management, guard against the collective community." He added: "Where they, correctional officers and police officers, feel they are misunderstood and that their work is too difficult, and too dangerous, and 'because no-one loves them', what they do is band together and they hide themselves behind the culture of not talking about it, because most of us [the public] don't understand."

The police educator talked in similar terms about police officer subculture. He talked about what he calls the 'musk ox syndrome': "You know about musk ox. They are large northern animals in the buffalo family. It's interesting, when they perceive themselves to be threatened they form a circle with the cows and the calves in the centre of the ring and all the bulls stand shoulder to shoulder with their massive heads out. And, oftentimes what happens is that the subculture within the police is the tendency to pull into a ring similar to that."

The former police officer continued to offer an explanation for this musk ox syndrome. The attitude of police officers, he said, is best characterized in this way: "The only people we can really trust, the only people we are really comfortable with is ourselves—other members of the subculture. So therefore I should pull into the subculture and don't blame me if I don't talk to you." In expanding further on police attitudes towards the public, he added: "We don't want you to like us, we don't want you to know, or we don't want to know that you like us because it doesn't allow us to pull back into the circle so readily, so the more I can push you further away, the more comfortable I feel with being part of the subculture."

This kind of thinking is confirmed by researcher into police behaviour Jerome Skolnick (1975). He suggests that the authority police have over the public, and the danger they feel themselves to be in, causes the police to isolate themselves from the community and to look to one another for support. (p. 44)

Finally, Vernon Fox (1983) in his book *Correctional Institutions* offers a similar perspective with respect to the corrections context: "The staff tend to develop loyalty to 'prison people' to insulate them from intrusion or criticism from the outside community…." (p. 162).

Summary

This chapter continued to explore the discussion on officer subculture that we started in Chapter 4, by incorporating and considering the perspectives of correctional and police practitioners.

Their perspectives confirm the idea of officer subculture as one characterized by an unwritten, informal code of conduct influencing, if not governing, the conduct of officers at work. Chief among the norms of the code, as is the case with the criminal code, is the requirement to remain loyal to one's colleagues. The practitioners all talked about the probable and unpleasant consequences of disloyalty.

Links between officer and criminal subculture were confirmed. In addition to the loyalty norm, both groups tend to see the sex offender on the lowest rung of the offender ladder. A shared argot also appears to exist.

The practitioners confirmed that the officer subculture requires identified "enemies" for its continuing existence. These enemies were identified as the criminal element, the "bosses" and the public.

Reflections

Would you agree that members of a subculture are likely to bind together more closely if they have identified "enemies"?

What are your views on the discussion in this chapter with respect to officer subculture being anti-inmate, anti-administration and anti-public?

6

Tough Decisions

The way I see it, the bottom line for making decisions when there is peer pressure, is to ensure that you are happy with the decision for yourself, not for others.

— Journal entry. Justice student in ethics course.

After reading this chapter you should be able to

- Explain how subcultural pressures can sometimes affect the choices officers make
- Explain William Tafoya's concept of the **vortex**
- Explain how the roots of officer wrongdoing may reside in allegiance to the solidarity norm
- Identify two possible ways in which an officer's moral choices can adversely affect his sense of personal and professional well-being

The Perils of Unthinking Loyalty

Permit me to stick my neck out a country mile (as if I haven't stuck my neck out already!). I suggest to you that the solidarity norm of police and correctional officer subculture constitutes fertile ground for officer wrongdoing. I am *not* suggesting that because police and correctional officer subculture is characterized, among other norms, by the solidarity norm, all officers are therefore wrongdoers. As we have suggested in earlier chapters, individual officers have found ways to maintain a sense of personal autonomy in spite of the subcultural norms. There is little doubt that most officers are honest and professional in the way they carry out their responsibilities.

What I am suggesting, however, is that it is not unusual, on those rare occasions when an individual officer or group of officers are adjudged to have acted unprofessionally, to discover that the solidarity constraint may have played some part in the initial wrongdoing, and almost certainly in any subsequent wrongdoing relating to the original incident.

Let me give you some police and corrections examples. We will look first at the policing context.

This incident we are going to discuss took place on a small police force of approximately 100 sworn officers in a small Canadian city of about 65,000 people. Three off-duty officers had attended a party. All three had been drinking. They were driving home in the early hours of the morning and the intoxicated driver, a little less drunk than his two partners, crashed the car. The accident scene (there were minimal injuries) was attended by a police officer who, of course, was a colleague of the three intoxicated officers. The four devised a "story" that the car had been driven by the wife of one of the officers, and that she had wandered off dazed and confused after the accident. The investigating officer, knowing the story to be false, nonetheless wrote in his notes that the three officers had been passengers in the car—that none of them had been driving it. The truth subsequently came out and the officers were reprimanded. Here is a case of an investigating police officer, knowing the lawful and proper action that should be taken under the circumstances, deciding in the interests of protecting his colleagues to do the wrong thing.

It is perhaps difficult to stand in judgment over him. What is a colleague supposed to do? To act ethically and professionally in this case might well have caused him subsequently to be labelled as disloyal, as a "rat," as someone not to be trusted by colleague officers. He found himself between the proverbial rock and hard place.

Mark Baker (1985) in *Cops* recounts an interview with a police officer who talks about how he and five other officers were called out to a domestic situation. "One kid moved over to one of the cops and said something to him. The cop pulled his gun, shot the kid in the head and killed him. Outright. Now you've got five cops standing there and going 'Holy shit, why did you do that for?'....They all got together and they figured, 'We got to do something. We'll say the kid had a gun or a knife or....' They come up with all these stories....Nevertheless, these cops felt that kind of bonding relationship with him to protect him. So they all lied. They didn't have to say that kid had a gun. But they wanted to protect their brother, because he was one of them." (pp. 199-200)

Here is a case of police officers, holding positions of public trust, being prepared to lie for each other even when by doing so they knew that justice would not be well served.

Here is one more example. It is not a "heavy-duty" example like the one above but I include it here because it speaks to how trainee police officers can be introduced to the subcultural norms. A police education student, after attending a police ethics seminar I had conducted, asked if he could speak with me privately. He said he was troubled. He had just completed a three-week practicum and his coach officer was a twenty-year veteran of the police force with which the student was placed. On one shift, he and the coach officer were told to go and ask some questions of a particular community resident. When they got to the house they discovered that no-one was home. The house was situated in the country and around it were several outbuildings. The officer decided to walk around the property and look in the outbuildings even though he neither had a search warrant, nor could justify obtaining one. They looked in one of the buildings and saw a van that they discovered was unlocked. The police officer opened the door to take a look at the serial number and found that a piece of paper had been placed over it. The van had obviously been stolen. The police officer said to the student: "Did you see a piece of paper over that serial number?" The question clearly was asked in such a way that the student was supposed to reply something like "What piece of paper?" In essence the police officer was trespassing and acting illegally, and now he was going to lay a charge of theft against the resident. But it was important to him that he could rely on the student. He said: "When this gets to court it is very important that you back me up and you say that the serial number was visible."

What if this trainee had said that he would have difficulty doing that? What if he had questioned the actions of the veteran officer? One doesn't have to be a rocket scientist, I think, to recognize that the trainee is in a difficult situation here. If he assures the coach officer that he can be counted on, he has in essence taken the first step toward—if not down—a slippery slope. If he indicates that he cannot make that promise to back up the officer in court, then he puts his future in policing in jeopardy because he will be seen as someone who is not solid and who, therefore, cannot be trusted.

(As an aside, there is a significant message here for senior officers when they select coach officers, and for coach officers once they have been selected. Rookie officers emulate the behaviours of coach officers; they pick up quickly both the good habits and the bad ones. Coach officers have a tremendous responsibility to perform at their best when being shadowed by a new officer. In a similar vein, police managers have a great responsibility to select coach officers wisely because of their potential for influencing their protégés).

Now let me give you some examples from corrections. The following account was given to me in one of my research interviews. I include the account in its entirety because it delivers a poignant message.

This inmate was a real bad actor on this particular living unit where I was working at the [identity withheld] Detention Centre and he ended up there. I watched him, and many of the staff had talked to me about him. I was the supervisor on the floor. And many of the staff over a period of days had talked to me about him and let me know that this guy was a trouble-maker. They couldn't catch him, but they knew he was causing trouble and creating a lot of tension.

He was picking on some of the black inmates; he was a white inmate himself, he was a big heavy guy, he was very strong, he was very muscular, and it looked like he controlled the unit.

One day I was walking past the corridor and I saw him cleaning outside the cells but in the day area where inmates would normally come out and watch television, play cards, and listen to the radio. All the other inmates were in their cells, but this particular officer had this guy out sweeping and mopping. This guy went to the cell of one of the black inmates, the inmate who was in his cell was no problem to us at all, he was very cooperative, doing his time, awaiting his trial, but he was also very big, about the same size as the other character I'm talking about. The cleaner went up to this guy's cell, the inmate inside the cell came to the grill and the cleaner—I watched the whole thing myself—spat at the black inmate on the inside, but there was plexiglass in between so it trickled down the glass. I immediately called for backup.

I had already made the decision this was inappropriate behaviour, there was no cause for this from my observation, and I was moving him to segregation. You understand that I had lots of information prior to this. The staff had serious concerns about him and the tension caused by him. It was one example for me that I could use to put him in segregation, to take him out of the unit and maybe solve some of the tension. So I called for backup and about seven staff came to the living unit. I told them to wait around the corner and I went with one officer who unlocked the doors for me and I called this guy out, and he said, "Where am I going?" and I said, "I want to talk to you out here." I eventually coaxed him out into the corridor and he said, "Where am I going?" and I said, "You are going to segregation because I just saw you spit at that guy in his cell." He threw these big arms up and said, "There's no fucking way, I'm not going anywhere," and I thought he was going to hit me because his arms had come up and then I lunged with my hands to grab his arms and lean against him on the glass. Just then all these seven other people came flying around the corner and the dance was on for them. What they saw, it appeared to me, was an opportunity to take out all their historical anger from the last two or three days, and they were kicking him, they were punching him, and they were pulling his hair.

It was, in my estimation, a very clear case of assault versus restraint. All they had to do was restrain this man but the vented anger unloaded and it was all I could do as a supervisor to stop it. I was yelling and screaming, I was grabbing legs and pushing people back, and it was a very uncomfortable situation for me. This guy was beaten up and I got him to segregation, left him in his handcuffs and leg-irons for a little while before I would go in and talk to him, because he was pretty angry. He didn't report it. I didn't report it as a physical assault.

This officer then talked about how he felt about the situation and the role he had played in it:

> Was it unethical? Absolutely. Did I do anything about it? Absolutely not. He was placed on a misconduct and in his adjudication he didn't say anything about it, I didn't say anything about it, so the facts of the intervention never surfaced.
>
> This is an example of somebody—me in this case—of somebody who bought into the officer subculture and didn't want to get seven staff dragged through a carpet of suspensions and investigations. Now had the inmate said that he wanted to report it [the abuse] I think I would be here telling you a story about someone who had lied, who heard the inmate's allegations but went and defended himself and seven other people. It [the subculture] is a very powerful pressure.

Let me give you another example in the corrections context, details of which were relayed to me by a justice educator who had worked for many years in correctional institutions. He said: "There was this situation where this inmate came in, was being admitted to the institution and this inmate was being very abusive to the officer, was very antagonistic okay, and the officer lost control. The officer assaulted the inmate. The officer came to me and said what he had done. And I said to him this is what you are going to write up." I asked the educator if the reports they wrote were fabricated. "It was a lie," he replied. He then said he had punched the officer to make it look like he had been attacked by the inmate. In this way the cuts and bruises on the inmate could be explained: there had been an altercation. "When I took that officer into the elevator I said 'You know what, we are going to make it look like this inmate attacked you. Close your eyes and I am going to punch you.' And that is exactly what I did."

In the policing examples, I included one incident involving a trainee police officer. The following similar example involves a trainee correctional officer.

An inmate was admitted to a detention centre to await trial on charges of having had sexual intercourse with a two-year-old child. One of the officers decided this was such a despicable offence that he was going to exact some measure of revenge for it. He went into the inmate's cell, picked up the Gideon Bible and hit the inmate in the face with it. The inmate's eye was cut, and subsequently swelled shut. Several officers, including the trainee officer, were in the vicinity and witnessed the assault. Later when a lieutenant was investigating the incident, each officer, including the trainee, were asked what they knew of the incident. They all knew what had happened but denied having any knowledge. The trainee later recounted to me that the decision for him was a no-brainer—there was no way he was going to tell the truth because it would have been too costly for him. In all likelihood, his future in corrections would have come to a grinding halt had he broken ranks and told what he saw.

One of my students, who completed his four-month field practicum in a maximum security correctional institution, recounted in an ethics class an experience he had had. He was standing in a corridor mainly housing black inmates. He overheard one of the officers telling one of the inmates that he was a "fucking nigger" and that "he was no better than a monkey in the zoo." The inmate group, as one might expect, erupted. The commotion drew the attention of the sergeant who went into the range to quiet down the inmates. According to the student, the sergeant first whispered something into the ear of the officer, and then proceeded to ask the inmates to be quiet. He appeared to chastise the officer for what he had said. The inmate group quieted down and the sergeant and the officer left the range together. Outside, and within earshot of the student, the sergeant said to the officer: "You're right, they are a bunch of fucking monkeys— I had to pretend to be telling you off in there or they would never have been quiet. Let's forget the whole incident."

The agony of the student who witnessed this incident still haunts me several years later. The student was deeply disturbed by this incident but chose to do nothing about it. In a journal written during the ethics course that I was teaching, he wrote: "I know that I should have spoken up to the lieutenant on duty and told him that I heard the officer make the two racial statements. However, I hesitated because I was scared that it would jeopardize my hard-earned respect with the officers. I am greatly disappointed with myself for not doing what my conscience wanted me to do. I feel that I have contributed to the racial problem by not doing what I knew was the right thing to do."

The pressure to conform, as one former officer put it, is a very powerful pressure.

These are examples of tough situations for officers, whether they are trainees or veterans. How can we expect officers to be their own persons under such circumstances? Might we be expecting too much of them when we say that we would like them to do the right thing? We shall return to these difficult questions later in the chapter.

At the time of writing, there is a "joke" making the rounds of the corrections system in my province—one that one of my students told me is related to all new staff and field practicum students. The joke carries with it a message that seems to fit the examples I have given.

> *Question*: How many correctional officers does it take to push a young offender down the stairs?
> *Answer*:   None. He fell.

Now it would be inappropriate to suggest that the kind of brutality depicted here in any sense characterizes the behaviour of correctional officers or police officers. Perhaps this is an illustration of the kind of black humour that often marks the conversation of correctional officers. Nonetheless, there is an implied message here—troubling one that it is—that all officers, including trainees, on occasion witness an incident but report something different, in the interests of protecting each other.

These are just a few examples of how our judgment can become obscured, and how the moral choices we make can be seen—at least retrospectively, if not at the time—to be faulty.

With respect to incidents where excessive use of force is the issue, one officer I interviewed asked rhetorically: "Are you holding that guy down a little bit longer to gain approval from your fellow workers? Are you using excessive force for that approval, for that acknowledgment, 'you're all right, you're one of us'?"

These are searching questions but it is important to ask them, for they centre on aspects of our value system concerning how we treat other human beings.

Reflections

If you had been the first police officer on the scene in the example of the three police officers who had crashed their car, how do you think you would have dealt with your colleagues' request to help them out of the "jam"?

"Rookie officers emulate the behaviour of coach officers; they pick up very quickly their good habits and the bad ones." What are your views on this statement?

All of the examples related above are examples of officer wrongdoing. Officers found themselves responding in ways that, privately perhaps, they would regret. Why is it, do you think, that occasionally we find ourselves behaving differently when we are with others than we might if we were alone?

Does the fact that you are dealing with an accused person who is alleged to have committed a particularly despicable crime mean that the normal rules of professional conduct can be temporarily suspended?

The Moral Struggle

In some of the examples discussed above, the officers involved actually admitted to knowing that their conduct could probably not be justified. In the other examples, where we do not know what the officers were thinking, would it also be a reasonable assumption to say that in all probability they knew that what they were doing could not be justified?

To think of the purpose of ethics education in the justice system as an activity designed to help officers know what is right or wrong, is, in my view, a redundant exercise. There may be some isolated cases in which, either because of moral bankruptcy or the gradual blunting of moral sensibility, an individual has lost sight of what is right and wrong. Generally, however, officers know what the right thing to do is in most given situations. The purpose of ethics training, then, rather than being an attempt to determine what is right and what is wrong, may be an attempt to help officers with their struggle when they experience personal moral conflict either when working alone or in their colleague group. Such a purpose can only be realized, I think, if the ethics educational experience is one characterized by empathy on the part of all concerned—teacher and student alike. If the experience is one in which participants feel they are being judged or manipulated, this would be a prescription for failure—painful to both teacher and student.

Let me offer an idea not generally discussed in any literature that I have encountered. I would suggest that an individual officer's sense of well-being or self-esteem can be positively or adversely affected by how he responds to these moral struggles. I would further suggest that there is a link between how an officer deals with moral conflict and the stress an officer can subsequently experience. Though I can offer no empirical evidence, there is some anecdotal evidence supporting my view, arising out of the interviews I have conducted and from what several ethics seminar participants have confided to me. Additionally, one or two writers have touched obliquely on the subject. I am going to expand on my idea in the hope that the discussion will become a topic of personal thought and class debate for you and your student colleagues.

Ethics education, therefore, can be seen in terms of its usefulness as a stress-reliever—as an aid to an officer's sense of well-being. It may also be seen as an aid to an officer reaching retirement relatively unscathed by major career incidents.

It is important that we keep this conversation in perspective. It is not being suggested here that officers encounter these crucial moral dilemmas on a regular basis. These are the more significant moral struggles that may be experienced only occasionally during an entire career. But, as few as they may be, they can be defining moments. How they are responded to can, to a large extent, establish the tenor of the individual officer's professional and personal life. Persistent irritability, relationship breakdown, alcoholism, tarnishing of reputation, loss of colleague respect, or loss of job are just a few examples of what can happen to an officer if found guilty of responding inappropriately to a moral struggle. And any or all of these effects, if experienced, can have a detrimental effect on an officer's general state of health.

We referred earlier to researchers Elizabeth Grossi and Bruce Berg (1991). They wrote a journal article called "Stress and Job Dissatisfaction Among Correctional Officers: An Unexpected Finding." Interestingly, in the context of discussing correctional officer stress, they refer to six stressors, one of which is "that one cannot always act the way either one would choose to, or the way the public might expect them [sic] to." This suggests to me the idea of moral conflict and moral struggle. It is significant that these two writers connect this struggle with the potential for stress. They add: "Again, it may be that in order to attain a satisfactory level of peer support, and reduce conflicting pressures endemic to correctional institutions, correctional officers must compromise their personal values and interests." (p. 80) Such compromise, if experienced, would constitute a fair amount of personal stress for most of us—would it not?

One of my university philosophy teachers, Clive Beck (1991), used to talk about how our value system and our ability to follow it can have an effect on our sense of well-being, or what he called the "good life." If we lose touch with our basic values, he suggests, our enjoyment of life can be impaired. I remember Beck differentiating between *moral values*, which he listed as carefulness, responsibility, courage, self-control, reliability, truthfulness, honesty, fairness, unselfishness, and *social and political values*, such as peace, justice, due process, tolerance, participation, cooperation, sharing, loyalty, solidarity, citizenship. (p. 3) You will notice that "loyalty" and "solidarity" are listed as two of the social and political values. And worthy values they are—in the right context. But what if they conflict with other values? What if, as a result of embracing loyalty and solidarity as values above all others, the result is a diminishing of individual courage, or truthfulness, or fairness, or honesty, or justice, or tolerance, or due process? If the latter values matter, and clearly they do for most correctional or police officers, there is going to be conflict and struggle, where one's decisions may well have a direct effect on one's sense of well-being.

My former teacher has a rather unusual way of looking at morality, and makes the point that it is generally unhelpful to blame people or to make them feel guilty for their choices. Rather, he sees a person's immorality as a problem for that individual, something that reduces well-being. He sees such people as unfortunate because they lack the motivation (and courage?) to do what is best for themselves. (p. 11) So it would not be too much of a stretch to link the idea of ethics education as it relates to helping us deal with moral conflict, with the successful management of stress in our professional lives.

One of my ethics course students wrote a comment in her journal that impresses me for its honesty, but at the same time troubles me because it shows poignantly how she has great difficulty dealing with her moral struggles. "I know that I don't always do what is 'right' though I have a sense of what that 'rightness' is," she writes. "It is a constant source of disappointment to me, and I can't seem to rise above it. It's horrible to know what the proper moral stance is and not have the strength to take it. This is another reason for my self-dislike." Clearly, here is an example of a person who is paying a fairly significant personal price for her moral struggle and for what she considers to be her lack of moral courage. She typifies, I think, what Beck means when he says that a person's immorality is a problem for that person.

Rhetorically, this person then asks in her journal a searching question: "Are those who don't see anything wrong with an unethical position happier than those who know the difference, but can't take a stand?" If my former teacher is correct in his thinking, the answer to this question is 'yes.' It is only at the point where we have a good idea about what we should do, but feel we can't do it, that the serious, health-harming conflict can begin to trouble us. The personal stress begins precisely at that point when we know what we should do, but feel that we do not have the moral courage to do it. Often, I would suggest, our courage is lacking because we fear the consequences of taking a stand. And what I have heard consistently from officers is that what they perceive to be moral failure on their part comes with a price.

One correctional officer trainee referred to this issue of moral courage when he said: "Do you stand alone and become a leper or do you let peer pressure and group think compromise your ethical stand? This is a hard question when you have to feed your family." There is, of course, no easy answer to this question. This person's concern is a legitimate one.

These uncourageous responses, often precipitated by the very real fear of reprisal, can cause many of us (myself included) to respond to the moral struggle by taking the safest route, the route of least resistance. As a result, the decisions we often make are ones that we would prefer not to make if we were stronger. We often take the route that we think will cause us the least amount of grief with our peer group. And often we neglect to think of the private angst that may result from the moral choices we make, and how that may impact on our sense of well-being—on how we feel about ourselves as persons.

Gail Sheehy (1977), in her book *Passages: Predictable Crises of Adult Life*, sees true adult development in the achievement of what she calls "autonomy," and "self-sufficiency." (pp. 52-56)

But this is a difficult enough goal to achieve in our "regular" lives away from the job. It is a much more difficult goal to achieve for police and correctional officers who can be influenced by the subcultural constraints of loyalty to colleagues.

In Chapter 1, reference was made to the Somalia inquiry in Canada. That inquiry into the killing of a Somali youth by some Canadian soldiers on a peacekeeping mission, has become characterized, I think many would agree, by what appears to be stonewalling and a conspiracy of silence on the part of many of the witnesses. In addition, many attempts have been made by the military to discredit the physician who was the first person to raise a concern about the way the youth died. The physician appears to have shown great moral courage, while many other witnesses have not. It is possible the others have not because they fear that they will have to endure ostracisation and discrediting similar to that experienced by the physician. But the physician was able to summon the courage to expose what he considered to be a wrongdoing.

What enables some individuals to risk everything to take a moral stand? One writer, Thomas Lickona (1976), a social psychologist, asks a similar question: "What enables a person to maintain moral perspective in the face of strong situational pressures?" (p. 124) I guess if we could answer that question we would all probably be much stronger in the face of moral conflict. One prolific writer in the area of morality, Lawrence Kohlberg (1984), thinks part of the answer may lie with what particular "moral stage" an individual has achieved. Kohlberg talks about six stages ranging from stage one—representing an unthinking, undisciplined moral sense—to stages five and six—representing what Kohlberg calls "principled moral thought." (pp. 454-459)

Thomas Lickona (1976), in an article "What Does Moral Psychology Have to Say?", refers to a U.S. soldier in the Vietnam War. You may remember the My Lai massacre during which an entire village was burned and many of its inhabitants, including women and children, were torched by U.S. soldiers. The soldier's name was Michael Bernhardt, and he was the only soldier who refused to participate in the massacre. He was found to be operating at a high stage in Kohlberg's definition of moral reasoning, and here is a statement Lickona attributes to him: "The law is only the law, and many times it is wrong. It's not necessarily just, just because it's the law. My kind of citizen would be guided by his own laws. These would be more strict in a lot of cases, than the actual laws. People must be guided by their own standards, by their self-discipline." (p. 125)

You will notice there is no sense of blind allegiance in this statement. When one considers what the pressure must have been like for Bernhardt to conform with the rest of his highly trained soldier colleagues, it is amazing that he was able to remain his own person.

Of course, you may ask what kind of army would one have if all soldiers danced to their own drummer! What would happen to the *esprit de corps* so essential to a group of soldiers fighting together?

Keep in mind here that we are discussing situations *in extremis*, as it were; situations that cause a significant crisis of conscience in an individual. Generally, you can still have your togetherness and solidarity and camaraderie—but only up to the point beyond which an individual would betray her sense of morality.

I remember reading a newspaper article in Australia entitled "Why loyalty is a two-way street." One question posed by writer Adele Horin was: "Is a loyal Nazi better than a disloyal one?" She made the point that loyalty "can blind you to higher loyalties, to truth-telling, justice, the common good." After pointing out that loyalty to a group can blind us to what she calls "wider commitments and obligations," she adds: "For example, the Blue Wall of Silence around police is a wall of loyalty and fear that keeps buddies true to each other at the expense, sometimes, of the good name of the force." (*The Sydney Morning Herald*, July 9, 1994). It is significant that she uses the word "fear" here. The fear, presumably, would be that of being ostracised by the group.

One of my current students, as I write this chapter, has a brother on a Canadian police force. His brother has told him that the worst thing that can happen to a police officer in his professional life is to be ostracised by his colleagues. It would demand considerable courage to take the kind of stand Michael Bernhardt took.

But let's return to this idea that *not* being courageous can sometimes, in a real sense, have an equally devastating effect on us and our careers. William Tafoya (1995), in an article called "Ethics and the Realities of Life: Surviving the Vortex," graphically depicts how one police officer got caught up in what Tafoya calls a "vortex": a kind of whirlpool that swallows or consumes everyone caught up in it. The incident he refers to is one in which a group of police officers in a major metropolitan police department were terminated for their part in the beating of a black motorist and the subsequent cover-up. One of the terminated officers spoke with Tafoya about the event several years later, and much of the article is a verbatim account of the interview. The article is a gripping, and sobering, account of what can happen to an otherwise good, but uncourageous person. In his introduction,

Tafoya expresses something amounting to incredulity that an otherwise good and intelligent officer would feel compelled to lie. This was the case despite the fact that the officer had come from a solid upbringing in which values and doing the right thing had been highly prized, and the fact that he knew that he was doing was wrong. Tafoya points out that even though this officer felt the cover-up was going to fail, he "nonetheless believed he must go along with the attempt to do so." (p. 576)

We clearly do not have the space here to include the long transcript (which in my view ought to be mandatory reading for every police officer), but I do think it important to include some of what the former officer said to Tafoya. In the transcript of the interview, Tafoya notes in several places where the former officer either began to, or actually lost, his composure. Keep in the mind that the incident had taken place several years earlier, and that he had made a relative success of his life after policing. Despite this, it is clear that he had suffered severe emotional and psychological pain at the time of the incident and in the ensuing years. Here are some of the things the former officer said:

> Yes. [in response to a question about the potential for retaliation from colleagues] This goes back a long way, before I joined the police department. I was socialized early and often in the police culture by friends who were police officers. From them I heard repeatedly that the most important lesson to be learned was sticking together. One friend [Fred], suggested that if I ever saw anything that I thought was improper—and was a rookie—I should keep quiet, go back to the car, and make like I was writing a report; stuff like that....A woman in our training academy class had previously done an internship with the department's Detective Bureau....We asked her about what it meant [the expression 'Hand-up guy']. She said rather sarcastically that 'Hand-up' is the worst insult one police officer can give another. A 'Stand-up' cop is one who covers for a fellow officer. Everybody likes such officers, trusts them. Such officers go to bat for one another. But a 'Hand-up' cop is likely to tell the truth and not cover for a fellow officer. It was then that I first began to understand that in the police culture, telling the truth was not always a virtue.

You will have noticed that these sentiments in a real way echo much of what we have been discussing in the book to this point. Now let's take a brief look at some of the things this fellow had to say about the effects on him personally of his inability to take a moral stand.

> I grew up in a little Christian Reformed community. I'm a religious person. I know what the truth is. I know you are supposed to be honest. That is probably what has bothered me more than anything else. I know what I did was

wrong. I knew it was wrong when I did it. I was sick with myself; still am....
To this day I struggle with this....Oh God (becomes very emotional). What I did,
I'm still ashamed of what I did. A comment a good friend made still haunts me.
He said, 'Integrity is like virginity. Once you lose it, it's gone.' (begins to cry).
It's been a lot of years; that's an awful long time. I don't think as though I've
got closure yet. I don't think I am going to wake up and find out it was all a bad
dream. It happened and I'm still having problems with it'. (pp. 577-580)

In my view, this is a graphic and disturbing account of how an otherwise principled officer, in the interests of being seen by his colleagues to be a "stand-up" officer, was prepared to put at risk, if not lose, everything he valued in life, including his reputation and career. For many of us, as for this former officer, such an experience would certainly result in a health-harming loss of self-respect. Indeed, at one point in the interview the former officer said that the primary reason for his agreeing to the interview was to try to come to terms with the whole issue. "That's why I'm letting you do this to me [the interview]," he said. "This is a catharsis for me. I've gotta stop somebody else, some other police officer, from doing this. I don't want somebody else to go through what I did." (p. 583)

Of course, one big question that has yet to be addressed is, "What if we make a decision that to be ostracised by colleagues would be more stressful than anything else that can happen to us?" This is a question that needs to be asked, and one we will address in Chapter 7. The former police officer in Tafoya's interview was asked what police departments could do to help officers like him who essentially open themselves up to becoming corrupted by responding in inappropriate ways because of subcultural constraints. One disturbing expression he used to describe his dilemma was, "I guess I was damned if I did, and I was damned if I didn't." (p. 580) This important issue will also be addressed in Chapter 7.

One final thought on the discussion in this chapter specifically, and in the book generally up to this point. There have been times during the process of writing this book that I have felt compelled to complete it because of certain "events" that occurred during its writing. One such event occurred two days ago. I had just returned from a two-week trip overseas and there were several messages waiting for me on my voice-mail at the college. One message was from a former student who is now working in corrections.

"I am phoning to apologise to you, John," began the call, "because when you taught us the ethics course I did not accept what you said to us that there may be moments in our career when we would find it very difficult to make the right decision. I always felt that I would never experience such difficulty because I was convinced that I would always be able to do what I thought was the right thing, that there would be no question about it. Well, I'm phoning to tell you I was wrong, and I want to apologise to you for not believing you. I am now confronted by a situation at work where, if I do what I think I should do, I will lose my job. So I just wanted to apologise to you and to say you were right in what you said in class."

Now it doesn't matter to me whether what I said in class was "right" or not. I was simply attempting to get the students to think about issues of professionalism and moral responsibility. What I did find upsetting was the tone of voice of the student. She did not leave a phone number and I do not know where she is working, so I have been unable to return her call. She is clearly struggling with the problem in a way, it seems to me, that is adversely affecting her life.

The personal price we can pay in attempting to deal with our moral struggles can be a significant one. And this is where, in my view, ethics education approached in an empathetic way may be of some help.

Reflections[3]

Would you agree, for the most part, that officers know what they should do in most situations, and that, if ethics education is geared to teaching what is right and wrong, it might be a redundant activity?

What is your view of the idea that our general sense of well-being as individuals is connected to how we resolve our moral struggles? What is your experience?

Have you ever considered how you would deal with a situation in which loyalty to colleagues may conflict with the values of justice, fairness or honesty?

Why is it, do you think, that individuals such as Michael Bernhardt are able to take a moral stand even when the consequences are likely to be painful?

Is a loyal Nazi better than a disloyal one?

A friend of the former police officer interviewed by William Tafoya said: "Integrity is like virginity. Once you lose it, it's gone." How do you react to this statement?

Summary

In this chapter we have suggested that the solidarity norm in officer subculture constitutes fertile ground for officer wrongdoing. We discussed some actual incidents both from corrections and policing to illustrate how this may be the case.

In the discussion it was suggested that officers, for the most part, know what is right and wrong, and that ethics education that is geared towards helping individuals know what is right or wrong is probably redundant. It was suggested that the purpose of ethics education should be to help officers cope with their moral struggles. As a result, on occasion officers may be able to avoid falling into a similar trap—or, to use Tafoya's term, "vortex"—to that in which the former police officer interviewed by Tafoya found himself.

One of the benefits of ethics education, then, is that directly or indirectly it can contribute to an officer's sense of well-being. That is to say, if an officer, as a result of an ethics education experience, manages to deal with her moral struggles in a personally satisfying way, her sense of self-esteem would be kept intact—if not enhanced. Of course, the converse would be equally true, as was so dramatically illustrated in the case of Tafoya's interview subject.

7

Tools for Moral Decision-making

I have always had the notion that we never truly think while in college. All we do is memorize.

— *Journal entry. Justice student in ethics course.*

After reading this chapter you should be able to

- *Explain why dilemmas are usually complex*

- *Explain why it is that however we respond to some dilemmas, we will feel that we are in a "no-win" situation*

- *Explain what is meant by the phrase "the choice really may be one between 'self-respect' and 'colleague respect'"*

- *Identify the two ideas that some officers have expressed that may help to explain how some officers deal with dilemmas they experience on the job*

- *Identify the seven "tools" that may help our decision-making when we are faced with a moral dilemma*

- *Explain why there may be a gender difference with respect to individual officers "setting limits"*

- *Explain what is meant by **setting limits***

- *Explain the principles of **benefit maximization** and **equal respect***

- *Explain what we mean by the **bell**, the **book**, and the **candle***

- *Explain what we mean by the **imaginary video camera***

- *Explain the general idea of **critical thinking***

- *Explain what we mean by **critical** in critical thinking*

- *Identify five elements of critical thinking*

- *Explain how thinking about moral stages may help our moral decision-making*

Introduction

By way of introducing the discussion on the tools of moral decision-making, consider two related ideas raised in the preceding chapter, one in the form of a question and the other in the form of a statement.

The question: "What if we decide that to be ostracised by colleagues would be more stressful than anything else that can happen to us?" (see page 89).

The statement: "I guess I was damned if I did, and I was damned if I didn't." It was expressed by the subject of William Tafoya's interview when describing the dilemma that led to his wrongdoing and subsequent dismissal as a police officer (see page 89).

The intrinsic nature of any dilemma is that it would normally beg no simple solution. If the issue confronting us is truly a dilemma then making a decision about it is probably going to be difficult. Sometimes even choosing to do what we consider to be the right thing does not necessarily mean that we are going to be completely at peace with our decision.

This would particularly be the case if we elected to make a decision that could implicate a colleague officer in some way. I think this is the kind of dilemma with which Tafoya's former police officer subject found himself confronted. If he had made a decision not to get caught up in the lying and fabrication, then in all likelihood he would have had to deal with the subsequent wrath and rejection of his colleagues. He would probably not be trusted again, and would have to endure the anguish of being labelled a "hand-up cop," and all that can go with that kind of labelling. On the other hand, having made a decision to stay solid, he experienced not only the public indignity of being fired as a crooked police officer, but also for many years has had to struggle, day in and day out, with his own personal demons arising from the incident.

No-win Situations

These kinds of situations often appear to be, in a very real sense, no-win situations. On the one hand, you can choose to stay solid, to be seen as a "stand-up cop," and continue to earn the acceptance, loyalty and support of your colleagues; on the other hand, you can choose to act according to the dictates of your conscience if it is leading you in another direction, and run the distinct risk of losing the acceptance, loyalty and support of your colleagues.

It would seem that the difference between the two choices is that you can opt either to continue to be admired and respected by your colleagues but lose some or all of your self-respect, *or* you can opt to hold on to your sense of self-respect but lose the respect of your colleagues.

Of course, there may be many occasions when the retention of both self-respect and the respect of your colleagues would be the result of your decision. I am not suggesting that all hard choices necessarily result in the "either this…or that" scenario. But there will almost certainly be times in your career as an officer when you will be confronted with the kind of dilemma we have been discussing here—with a choice that really is one between self-respect and colleague respect. And when these situations arise, they can, as we have discussed, be extremely difficult to resolve, and result in personal anguish.

It is at these moments that one's sense of self, and who one is as a person, is put squarely on the line.

Two Ideas

Perhaps it is appropriate to mention here, as an aside, that I have had some interesting conversations with officers about this topic. They have expressed two ideas that will perhaps provide interesting material for your personal thought or for discussion with your colleagues. Perhaps some of you may think these ideas worthy of exploration, and I would encourage you to do some further research on them.

We don't have time in the context of this book to discuss the ideas in detail, nor am I going to offer any comment on them, but here they are:

First, a few officers have suggested to me that some officers are able to cope with dilemmas that have the potential to put them at odds with their colleagues, simply by regarding loyalty to and solidarity with colleagues as the preeminent value in their professional lives. In other words, deciding that to abide by this principle is the ultimate morality. This one-dimensional thinking, of course, can enable individuals to get out from under some moral struggles that are essentially multidimensional in nature and which do not beg a simplistic solution. It may be an effective way of avoiding anguish for some officers. Whether or not this approach would count as an intellectually honest one is a moot point.

Second, some officers have suggested that when they are at work, because of the unusual nature of their job and the character of the socially deviant "clients" with whom they normally work, they can mentally and emotionally justify *suspending* the morality they operate by in their private lives. In other words, they can rationalize allowing themselves to be governed by a different, and somewhat questionable, morality on the job. If this does happen, it would seem here that one's moral sense is compartmentalized—that one's "real" moral sense is practised and adhered to in one's private life, where one remains committed to truth-telling and fairness, and so on; and that the other moral(?) sense in the workplace allows one to engage in what I call "means-end" morality, where the normal tenets of morality, such as the ones we have mentioned, can be suspended or ignored. I trust you will have some fun debating and discussing these ideas.

What is your view of the idea that to be ostracised by colleague officers for taking a moral stand might be one of the worst things that can happen to an officer?

If you were confronted by what you thought was a "no-win" situation, what factors would probably influence your decision-making? Attempt to "anchor" your response to a specific situation.

Is it reasonable to talk about "self-respect" and "colleague respect"? Or, does this way of thinking simply not recognize that, for the officer, the two are invariably linked?

What are your views on the two ideas expressed by officers as a way of explaining how some officers are able to deal with moral conflict?

Let's return to the topic under discussion. We have suggested how extremely difficult it can be to be confronted with a no-win situation. We are now going to discuss some "tools" we can use in our moral decision-making. We should come at those decisions understanding that there is seldom a perfect solution, and that there is probably going to be some pain whatever we choose to do in a given situation. The tools, hopefully, will enable us to make decisions that give us the greatest degree of comfort.

I guess one test of a decision we are wrestling with might be to reflect on it at three in the morning on a night of fitful sleep, and see how we feel about it!

If by using one or more of these tools you are helped to make the best possible decision for you and for others affected by that decision, then the time and effort you commit to considering them may be more than justified—at least in terms of your peace of mind and sense of well-being. More important, perhaps, thinking in this way may help at some point to save your career.

Seven Tools

1. Setting Limits

This is a technique that some officers have told me helps protect them from becoming caught up in potentially compromising situations. They simply indicate to colleagues, in a pleasant and courteous way, what their personal limits are. They may do this regarding, for example, using too much force, or gossiping, or sleeping on night shifts, or accepting gratuities, or whatever the case may be.

These questionable practices are simply cited as examples, and are not meant to imply that any one of them or a combination of them normally characterizes the behaviour of officers.

Setting these limits and making them known to colleagues can, I am told, cause a colleague who might be contemplating responding unethically to a given situation to have second thoughts about doing so in your presence.

An example might be a situation in which an officer partner on night shift tells you he wants you to "spot each other off" as you alternately take turns to sleep. You might say to him, by way of establishing your own limits, "I don't feel safe when either one of us is sleeping, so I would prefer it if we both stayed awake." If he tells you to take a running jump, so to speak, you may then say, for example, "I will not sleep, and I would prefer it if you did not. It is not safe. But if you continue to sleep I may be left with no other option but to take it further. I really do not want any unpleasantness between us, but the choice is yours." To set our own personal limits in this way can be difficult for us, but it can save an awful lot of grief later. What do you think?

Perhaps it should be added here that many of the officers who have advocated this technique have been women. My research shows clearly that female officers more than male officers use this technique effectively. We can hypothesize why this may be the case, and I hope that you will give some thought to the issue. The research also shows that when male officers are able to use this technique without running the risk of alienating their colleagues, they generally enjoy the comfort of being viewed by their colleagues as credible, experienced and reliable in an emergency. It could be problematic for a rookie officer to use this technique, especially if she is perceived by more experienced colleagues to be superior to them in some way. A new officer would have to set personal limits cautiously and diplomatically, otherwise he could be setting himself up for an interesting orientation to the job! This is not necessarily to suggest, however, that if you are a trainee officer you should not consider the advantages in adopting this technique.

Reflections

Is it realistic, do you think, for a new or relatively new officer to "set limits" with colleagues?

If you answered yes, what are the risks, if any?

If you answered no, try to explain why you feel this way.

Some male officers have expressed the view that they perceive themselves to be much more subject to the potential for what they call "parking lot justice" than are female officers. What do you think? What is your experience?

What is your view of the idea that experienced, proven officers are more able to set personal limits?

2. Ethical Principles

There are some writers who think, at those times when there is time to think (and I realize that this may not always be the case in corrections or policing), that it can be helpful to incorporate the consideration of certain ethical principles into our pondering a dilemma. Three university professors—Kenneth Strike, Jonas Soltis and Emil Haller (1988)—have written a book called *The Ethics of School Administration*. In the book they explain skilfully, and demonstrate, how incorporating some thought about ethical principles into our moral decision-making can help us arrive at more informed, and probably more correct decisions. In the context of this book we do not have the time, in any kind of depth, to discuss the practice, so I would recommend that you read the book if what follows is of special interest to you. The practice is what Strike et al. call "the application of principles to cases." (p. 4)

Let me caution, however, before we discuss the practice of applying ethical principles to resolving moral dilemmas. The ethical principles themselves can sometimes give us conflicting messages about what we should do in a given situation. A second caution would be that incorporating a consideration of the principles into our decision-making could potentially rationalize a decision with which we basically feel uncomfortable.

I would encourage you to practise using the principles in your own moral decision-making. One way to get used to incorporating them into your thinking would be to use them as you discuss the dilemmas in Chapter 8, and any other dilemmas arising from your own experience that you feel comfortable bringing to class for examination. There are two basic principles:

The Principle of Benefit Maximization

This principle holds that when we are faced with a conflict about what we ought to do about any given moral dilemma, we should attempt, prior to making any decision, to weigh the consequences of our decision. If we judge that one particular decision, among all the ones we could make, is likely to lead to the greatest amount of good for the greatest number of people, then this decision is the one, according to this principle, that we should make. The morality of our action, therefore, is judged against the probable consequences of that action.

This principle can be useful in helping us think through our moral dilemmas. However, of the two principles we are going to discuss, this is the one that is most problematic. We suggested earlier that sometimes these principles can give us conflicting messages about what we should do in a given situation. The principle of benefit maximization is the principle more likely to conflict with the other. This is a principle that can, unless we are careful, be used for the purpose of rationalizing decisions and behaviours about which we do not feel at peace or, more plainly put, which we suspect are wrong.

For example, a couple of police officers may apprehend a suspect who they have a strong instinct (but no proof) is at the root of a string of crimes that have been committed recently. The officers know from their experience that this particular suspect is a bad actor and that the community generally would be safer with him behind bars. You can see already that in a case like this it would be easy to use this principle of benefit maximization to justify, for example, planting drugs on this suspect, in the absence of the officers' being able to come up with any concrete evidence. In that way, they may convince themselves they have served the community well by making it a safer place. In other words a little bit of injustice has led, they convince themselves, to the greater good. Dubious means have led to a good end, so the wrongdoing is justified as well-intentioned and productive.

In the corrections context, correctional officers may feel that to beat a convicted child molester whom they feel has "got away" with a light sentence, may cause that offender to think twice about re-offending, again thereby rendering the community a safer place for children.

As reprehensible as child molestation is, we should think long and hard about whether, as peace officers, we have the right to suspend the normal rules of justice, law and order, in the course of our duties.

The kind of thinking and behaviour in the two hypothetical situations above would be difficult to defend, either morally or legally. Many would consider the officers' responses to be illegal and unprofessional. Others would consider them to be unethical, because the actions of the police officers and the correctional officers are the sorts of actions that would normally lead to cover-ups and dishonesty in the interests of self-protection.

Their actions may essentially represent a kind of vigilante justice; the thinking that governs these kinds of actions may not be much different from the thinking that governed lynch mobs.

For the last decade or so this utilitarian approach (another name given to this kind of thinking) to making moral decisions has been embraced to a great extent in the Western world, particularly in North America. But because of the tendency of individuals to use this sort of thinking for the purpose of rationalizing all kinds of questionable behaviours, it is now, in the late 1990s, being questioned as a useful aid.

My view is that although it is a useful concept to keep in mind, the principle of benefit maximization is more likely to help us in an objective way if used in conjunction with the second principle we are going to discuss. The two principles looked at together may serve us well as they provide checks and balances against any self-serving motives that may otherwise be lurking in our decision-making.

The Principle of Equal Respect

When we use this principle, rather than concentrating in our moral decision-making on the potential benefit of that decision to the greatest number of individuals, we concentrate much more on the appropriateness of considering all individuals as being worthy of equal treatment, simply because they are human. The humanity of individuals is the common denominator here rather than, for example, their cultural or socioeconomic status.

You can readily see that when we consider the two hypothetical situations we discussed in The Principle of Benefit Maximization section, and incorporated into our thinking the principle of equal respect, it would be difficult to continue to feel justified in taking the law into our own hands. Would we wish similar treatment to be handed out to our son, mother or grandparent? How would we feel if we were on the receiving end of such treatment? Would we wish people generally to be treated in this way?

I think we could make a reasonable assumption that most officers would respond to these questions in a way that would indicate they are committed to fairness and justice.

So we can see here, by stopping to consider this principle before we make a decision, our thinking about a particular course of action and our subsequent behaviour may be radically different than if we had not stopped and thought in this way. And, equally important, the danger can be reduced of falling into the potential trap of rationalizing an act that could get us into deep trouble.

If we think about it for a moment, it becomes clear that the notion of due process has its roots in this principle of equal respect, as does our thinking about the basic rights of individuals in the kind of society in which we live. The concept of due process, though a legal term, is very much a moral term also. As you know, the concept of due process has to do with developing and applying fair procedures for making important decisions affecting the lives of others. There is something ethical about such an approach. As a private citizen I take comfort from it, even though from time to time the process can let us down.

Reflections

Why should we be aware of the inherent dangers of using only one ethical principle to justify a decision?

Think of a moral dilemma you have encountered. How would you use either or both of the ethical principles to assist you in your decision-making?

Is an accused person or an offender entitled to benefit from the principle of equal respect?

Is it possible, do you think, to make a good case for sometimes suspending due process?

3. The Bell, the Book, the Candle

These are tools for moral decision-making that have been suggested by Michael Josephson of The Josephson Ethics Institute in California. They are simple and straightforward to use, but can be a most useful check against which to measure a course of action we are considering. I would suggest here—and this is a point that you may wish to think about for yourself and also to debate in class—that if we are contemplating doing something that we feel reluctant to subject to the scrutiny of tools like these, then we probably know already whether we should take that step. Our reluctance probably indicates what we know either instinctively or intellectually that what we are proposing to do is not morally justifiable.

The *bell* simply refers to a question we might ask ourselves when we are about to make a choice: "Are any warning bells going off?" If so, then we should at least stop and reconsider what we are proposing to do. Of course, the warning bells may be going off simply because of a particular way in which we have been socialized or conditioned, where the proposed course of action is still a defensible and ethical response. Normally, however, if the warning bells go off, and we wish to avoid for ourselves much subsequent grief, we would be wise to heed their warning and respond appropriately.

The *book* is a tool that simply refers to laws, regulations, codes of ethics and other forms of written guidance. So when I am contemplating a course of action there are a number of questions I can ask myself. Is what I am proposing to do lawful? Does it fall within the department's policies and procedures? Does it potentially violate any section of the department's Code of Ethics?

The *candle* simply refers to how the decision might look if it were exposed to the light of day, as it were, or to public scrutiny. If I choose to act in this way and it is examined in the public arena, can I defend my action? Will I continue to feel good about my action, and will I continue to feel justified in doing what I did?

Reflections

Is it possible to quickly review the bell, the book and the candle in heat-of-the-moment decisions? Or, are these tools only useful when considering moral conflicts, where making a quick decision is unlikely to be an issue?

Have you ever consciously used the bell, the book and the candle, or something approximating them, in your own moral decision-making?

If your answer is yes, was the exercise helpful as a guide in your decision-making?

4. The Imaginary Video Camera

We live in a technological age and one of the curses or blessings of this age—depending on one's perspective—is the video camera. Many unsuspecting souls, as we have seen on the news and in documentaries, have discovered to their great cost that they are the unwitting "stars" of video footage. And included among these unsuspecting souls, as many of you will have seen, have been a number of law enforcement personnel.

I am, of course, talking about those embarrassing moments when inappropriate conduct is captured by some amateur sleuth in the vicinity, armed with her video camera. For example, many of you reading this will remember the graphic video footage of the Rodney King beating by police officers in Los Angeles.

As I write this particular part of the book, on the news the other evening there was again graphic film footage of a police officer, having stopped an unarmed motorist for a traffic violation, inexplicably firing several shots at the driver who later died of his injuries. The driver was unarmed, and had stopped his car, at which point the officer appeared to lose his composure. Without the benefit of the video recording, most of us would have believed the officer's subsequent story that he had been attacked first.

Some interesting events unfolded in New South Wales, Australia, in 1996 and 1997. A royal commission was appointed to look into charges of widespread police corruption across the state. As part of the investigation, some police cars were bugged. Microscopic cameras were strategically placed in the dashboard of the cars. As a result, many illegal activities by police officers were recorded and later produced as evidence to the inquiry. One particularly unscrupulous and corrupt police sergeant, after telling a television news crew that he knew nothing of police corruption, was subsequently shown video footage of himself sitting in the driver's seat of his police car, counting out money he had just been paid by a drug dealer. The dealer was sitting in the passenger seat of the police car, as bold as brass, almost as though it were his office!

You will have heard the humorous expression "You know it's going to be a bad day when a reporter from *60 Minutes* taps at your door!" The police sergeant's experience of watching himself as his corruption was exposed for all Australians to see must have given new meaning to the expression.

These are just a few examples of how we can get caught out by the wonders of modern technology. It would be fair to say that you and I may also at some point find ourselves on the receiving end—having our movements and behaviours captured by a video camera without our permission. And that thought alone can be a useful deterrent to our behaving unprofessionally.

What I am suggesting here is that on those occasions when you or I are beginning to feel uncomfortable, either with what we are thinking of doing, or indeed are already doing, imagining that our behaviours are being recorded may help us to gain a clearer perspective. Thinking in this way may be a quick but useful check at that moment on whether or not our judgment, or our behaviour, or the action we are contemplating, is sound and defensible.

As you can readily see, this technique is an extension of the candle technique, in which we ask ourselves whether our actions can be justified in the light of day.

Is there a danger that in suggesting the imaginary video camera as a tool, I am playing on the emotion of guilt?

If you answered yes, is there a possibility that this could be construed as a manipulative move on my part?

If you think it might be manipulative, is the manipulation justified if it results in even one career being saved?

If you answered yes, why? If you answered no, why not?

(*Note*: You can see from these questions that this is an issue with which I wrestled prior to my making a decision to include the imaginary video camera as a tool).

5. Critical Thinking

Critical thinking is not so much a specific tool to help us with our moral decision-making, as a general approach to problem-solving that can also help us as we struggle with our moral dilemmas.

You will no doubt be aware, through your own reading and through some of the work you have done in your classes, of the concept called critical thinking. There are many books on the subject and I would encourage you to do some research and reading on the topic for yourself. In the context of this text we only have time to touch upon the skill.

You will notice that I use the word "skill" to describe the process of critical thinking. It is a skill that we can acquire through learning and discipline, but something that few of us come by naturally.

Briefly, then, what do we mean by the term "critical thinking"? First of all, the skill has little or nothing to do with being critical in the way we normally think of being critical. It doesn't mean we should go around criticizing. Rather, critical thinking means that we should refrain from taking any idea or point of view at face value; that we should examine it carefully before making a personal judgment about it. It means also that we should probably think twice about allowing others to do our thinking for us. It means that we should aim to think for ourselves, to weigh the relative merits and demerits of any idea, to be prepared to look at all sides of a given issue, and to come to our own informed opinion.

The task, however, is not an easy one. Our thinking in general, and the way we look at most issues specifically, is unclear at best, leading us often either to simply accept a point of view without examining it for ourselves, or to cling to our own—often blindly accepted or adopted—position on a given issue.

In the literature, you will find many variations on the theme of critical thinking. Put simply, critical thinking can be summed up in the following way. If we are critical thinkers,

1. we will resist the temptation to jump to conclusions about issues;

2. we will be prepared and able to think independently—that is, to think for ourselves;

3. we will have the courage always to be prepared to subject our own views and ideas to scrutiny by ourselves and others;

4. we will refrain from accepting blindly any point of view or idea that is offered, even (or especially!) if it is offered by someone we consider to be an expert;

5. we can demonstrate skills of reasoning that would include the ability to honestly weigh the evidence, to trust only reliable sources of information, to disregard hearsay or unsubstantiated opinions, and to think logically about an issue.

You can see that if I discipline myself to think in this way, my response to situations involving rumour, or gossip or peer pressure, for example, is probably going to be different from my response if I did not.

Let me share something with you that I tell my students. Keep in mind that it is a personal opinion of mine and I am more than willing for you to hold it up to scrutiny, to see whether there is any merit in it. I tell my students how I believe we often develop our value systems. I explain to them that on occasion we accept ideas and values from others—normally significant others, for example, parents, teachers, sports coaches, or our church or school leaders—and we put them on as we would an item of clothing. Just as we generally only put on clothing we like, we tend to accept the values we "like." The problem is that if indeed there is any truth in what I am saying, many of our values cannot be said to be truly our own. We have adopted them, as it were, without holding them up to careful examination.

In essence, it is something like building our values foundation on sand. Because they are not truly our own values, they can be readily shifted, or challenged or changed. Because these adopted values are not our own, our investment in them can often be shallow, causing them to become quite vulnerable to any wind of change.

Would you agree that the ability to think critically is a skill that must be learned?

What is your view of the idea that many of our opinions, beliefs, and even values, are simply adopted by us? That is, that we just inherit them without stopping to think about them for ourselves?

6. The Other Person's "Moccasins"

I remember seeing somewhere the Canadian native saying "Never judge another man until you have walked two moons in his moccasins." In more modern parlance, we might say that it is important to look at every situation from the respective points of view of the various stakeholders. Forgive my using the term "stakeholders" because I think it is one of those overused, clichéd expressions. It does convey, however, the importance of attempting to see the other person's point of view when we are trying to make sense of a complex situation.

Of course, this is no easy task, even when time permits. When speed of response is of the essence, it is an even more difficult task. The wise officer, however, is the one who at least makes the attempt to develop a sense of how all parties involved in an issue, and its subsequent resolution, come to see the issue and the "facts" surrounding it in different ways. Here are some questions we may be wise to ask if we are aspiring to arrive at a judgment bearing a reasonable resemblance to reality: What is likely to be influencing the accused person in terms of his explanation of the incident? What about the witnesses? Why is the shift sergeant interpreting the "facts" in the way she is? What about the crown attorney's perspective? Why are there some discrepancies in the witness accounts of what they thought they saw happen? What is their relationship, if any, to the accused, and is this likely colouring their perceptions of what happened? What would I be thinking and feeling if the roles were reversed, and I were in their shoes? What does my instinct tell me about this incident, and how does this relate to the facts as they unfold? Have I allowed myself to develop tunnel vision here? Am I so convinced of the "facts" as I see them that I am simply unprepared to take a step back to reconsider my reading of the events?

If we do become so convinced of our individual perception of what happened in a given situation, first, we are clearly not being mindful of the perceptual perils of claiming to know for sure what happened, and, second, we are covertly if not overtly claiming that we are the only individual capable of making the correct judgment!

Now I would not wish to suggest here that it is permissible or defensible to become paralysed by the fear of making a mistake. Some people may see such careful and informed decision-making as wishy-washy, or as fence-sitting. Let me disavow you of that notion. Decisions have to be made, and often they have to be made in a hurry. But jumping to conclusions based on one officer's personal perspective is generally not an approach that is going to lend itself to informed and wise decision-making.

A standard check might be asking something like, "How would I feel in this situation if I were this person? Am I looking at the entire situation, and am I responding to it in as objective a way as possible?

Attempting to put ourselves in the other person's moccasins might be one step in the right direction. By so doing there may be an enhanced chance that justice will be served.

Reflections

Can you think of any case where justice was not served because the investigating officers jumped to a premature conclusion about an accused person's guilt or innocence?

If you can think of such an incident, might the process described here of attempting to see the situation from many perspectives have helped to bring about a more appropriate and less embarrassing conclusion?

7. Moral Stages

One important figure in the area of moral development and moral education is Lawrence Kohlberg. I would encourage you to look up some of Kohlberg's work, and to engage your facilitator in a discussion about his ideas.

It is my hope that Kohlberg, although now deceased, will forgive me for reducing what can sometimes be fairly complex theories of moral development down to what can only be described as the most simplistic of levels. His work advocates that humans operate at any one of six stages of moral development. The stages range from 1, which is the least morally developed and principled, to 6, which is the most developed and highly principled stage.

If we are at stage 3, for example, he claims that the motivation for our behaviour comes from a need to conform, where relationships are critically important to us and govern our moral decision-making (ring a bell?). Stage 4 is the stage at which we make our choices based on what Kohlberg calls "conscience maintenance." If we don't feel guilty, we must be doing all right. Stages 5 and 6, on the other hand, are stages at what he calls the "post-conventional" level, where individuals are able to make reasoned moral judgments based on sound ideals and ethical principles, and where those individuals are more likely to have the moral courage to follow through on their moral choices.

Now what is the point of all this? (And I am sorry if this all sounds convoluted!) The point is that if we think of stages 3 and 4 as basically "going with the flow," and stages 5 and 6 as principled and courageous, we may ask ourselves an important question just prior to making a moral choice: If I make the moral choice I am about to make, at what stage might I be operating? Is my choice based more on what others think of me and what I think of them, or is my choice one that I can truly call my own and that is reasoned, principled and strong?

It's a tough question, but it can be a useful guide or check on our behaviour.

Reflections

At what stage do you think you generally operate in the ethical choices you make?

What do you understand from the term *moral courage*?

Putting the Tools to the Test

Let's have a go at working through a moral dilemma using the tools. We will do so briefly, but the process may take a little longer in class because of the diversity of opinion that no doubt will be brought to the issue.

As this chapter was being written, I had lunch with a chief of police, and during our chat he related a dilemma he had been thinking about. He said, "Geez, I've got this problem. We have some neighbours several doors up from us, and they are absolutely delightful people. We have known them for several years." He explained that the two families had socialized together. "Their son is a graduate from a college justice program, and desperately wants to get on with my force. But you know, I kind of have some reservations about him. There's something that I can't put my finger on, I feel kind of uneasy about him. Obviously his parents would like me to help because the kid has got his heart set on policing, but I don't know."

So, briefly, let's try to apply the tools to the problem. The dilemma is, should the deputy chief help his neighbour's son to get hired by his police department?

The first tool, setting limits, appears to have little or no direct application to this problem.

The second tool is ethical principles, the first of which is the principle of benefit maximization. Now if we apply this principle to the problem, we quickly see that the greatest benefit, if the lad were hired as a result of the deputy chief's influence, would accrue to the son and his parents. The fact that there may be a much better candidate available would mean that the interests of the community would probably not be well served. Overall, therefore, it is likely that less public good would result if the son were hired. The second principle, equal respect, refers to giving all individuals an equal amount of consideration. That would clearly not be the case if the deputy chief gave this lad an edge by exerting his influence. So far, then, the tools would indicate that the chief should not use his influence to help the neighbour's son.

The next tools we discussed were the bell, the book and the candle. In this instance, I am unsure about what the deputy chief, if he were to use his influence to help this lad, would say about the bell. Only he would know. The book, however, may be helpful. Police force policies would most certainly address issues of conflict of interest, the importance of fairness, and the inappropriateness of senior officers using influence for personal reasons. (This may mean, too, that warning bells would be going off.) The candle, referring to whether a decision will stand up to public scrutiny, would indicate that the deputy chief should not use his influence in this case. Clearly, most members of the public would wish that police hiring decisions would be based on fairness and equal opportunity. So far, so good: the deputy chief would be unwise to use his influence.

The next tool, the imaginary video camera, would probably also indicate that it would be unwise of the deputy chief to help his neighbours, because if his use of influence in this way were recorded or documented, he would probably have to answer some hard questions. The message continues to be that he should not help the lad any more than he is prepared to help any other candidate.

Critical thinking is the next tool. If the deputy chief is prepared to put his decision-making to the test he has already submitted himself to, he has begun to engage in critical thinking. He would now be beginning to see the issue much more clearly, and the decision-making process would be removed from the gut level, to a level where neighbourly loyalties are probably not going to dictate the decision.

When we consider the deputy chief placing himself in the other person's moccasins, an important question to ask might be, If I were a candidate for this police force and I thought I was placed at a disadvantage because of a senior officer's "pull," how would I feel? The answer would appear to be self-evident. Conclusion: the deputy chief should not use influence to help the neighbour's son.

Finally, can consideration of Kohlberg's moral stages help us here? Well, if the deputy chief wants to be liked, and wants to reinforce to an even greater extent his neighbourliness with the lad's parents, he can help the lad. But would this be a good reason? Perhaps a better way might be to think the whole thing through independently, and then make the decision that is the right one, irrespective of any potential fallout with the neighbours. Loyalties, therefore, would not be permitted to "colour" his thinking about the situation, nor to dictate his decision.

It would appear that the deputy chief can make his decision with confidence and move on. The agonizing is over. To use his influence in this case would probably be unfair, and would probably not withstand public scrutiny. And perhaps most important, the general good of the community would be better served by hiring the best candidate available.

My hope is that this little exercise will demonstrate how our moral decision-making can be helped by submitting the dilemmas we encounter to a similar process.

Summary

Perhaps the acid test underlying all of these "checks" is, How do I feel about myself? Do I feel strong? Or, do I feel awkward and ill at ease about my action? Do I feel shaky inside? Am I depressed about the choice I made? Do I find myself constantly looking for ways to justify my choice?

I think it would probably be safe to say that few of us, and I include myself here, have not experienced the soul-searching indicated by troubling questions like these.

The biggest worry of all, however, would be the person who has never felt this struggle, for none of us is perfect. The individual who has experienced the struggles can, at least, take some comfort from the fact that her moral sense is still active.

We are human, and part of being human means that we will make mistakes.

However, the mistakes may be fewer, and the really big, career-destroying and peace-of-mind-destroying mistakes may be fewer, if not eliminated, if we adopt some of these techniques to help us work through the moral dilemmas confronting us in our work.

These tools may help us think more clearly, and they may serve to reinforce our moral sense, but in the final analysis the entire issue boils down to one of moral courage. I know what I should do, because I have thought about the dilemma carefully and honestly, but do I have what it takes to follow through with what I think I should do?

Moral fortitude does not come easily or readily.

Let me leave you with one final thought in this chapter. Might it be the case that the courage to act may come more readily for having systematically, honestly and thoughtfully weighed the consequences of our decisions?

8 Where Do You Stand?

There is always more than one choice to be made. I do not think there are right and wrong choices, but rather better and not very good choices.

— Journal entry. Justice student in ethics course.

Introduction

As you can see, this chapter has no Chapter Objectives section. The purpose of this chapter is simply to give you some material for your own thinking, and for discussion with your classmates.

You may remember my stating in Chapter 1 that the dilemmas included in this chapter are based on actual experiences. They are not hypothetical. They have been directly or indirectly recounted to me by officers in the field, so I hope they will ring a few bells for you.

The police and corrections scenarios are not separated, and this has been done deliberately. You are encouraged, whatever justice profession you are studying for, to have a go at working through several, if not all of the issues. In this way you will develop some insights into the kinds of awkward problems that can confront both police and correctional officers.

When you are thinking about the dilemmas and how you or your colleagues would probably respond to them, attempt to place yourself in the actual situation. It is one thing, in the comfort of one's home or the relative comfort of a classroom, to imagine how we would respond. But I want you to try and transport yourself into the situation and imagine the dilemma unfolding. Try to grasp all of the nuances of the situation: the subtle and not-so-subtle pressures, the friendships, the comradeship, the expectations you have of yourself. Think about who you are as a person. Think about the faith your parents and family probably have in you. Look at each situation in its entirety and attempt to weigh all the factors before you begin working out what you think you would do.

Let me offer a word of caution. If you read a dilemma and you think you know immediately what you would do, there is a good chance that you have not grasped the complexity of the issue. They are dilemmas because they are likely to induce in you a similar response to the one experienced by William Tafoya's subject: "I guess I was damned if I did, and I was damned if I didn't."

Please also be aware that thinking we know what we *should* do in a given situation, and thinking we know what we *would* do in that situation may be two different things. If there is a discrepancy like this between your thinking and your anticipated behaviour, what might account for the discrepancy? Why is it, do you think, that at times even when we know fairly certainly what we should do, we can find ourselves lacking the moral courage to follow through?

So here are the dilemmas. Some relate to police officers, others to correctional officers, and others to both professions. One scenario asks you to consider a dilemma facing a senior officer, so that you can begin to realize how difficult it can be at times for administrators when they, like you, have to wrestle with what should be done.

As you wrestle with them, practise using the tools discussed in Chapter 7. Have fun with them. But at the same time remember that one of these days you may find yourself in a similar situation for real. I hope the experience of thinking both privately and publicly about them, and discussing these dilemmas with classmates, will help you when the time comes.

You should not feel "led" in any direction by the questions. They are not designed to move you toward thinking in a prescribed way about an issue. They are included simply as prompts for thought and discussion. What matters most of all is what you think and feel about these issues, whether or not you can defend your position on them, and what reasons you employ to support your response.

Try to remember what I said in an earlier chapter about moral courage beginning where we are willing and able to take a hard, honest look at dilemmas like these; and where we are strong enough, at least for a few minutes, to put aside our prejudices, biases and preconceived notions, and honestly face up to the hard questions.

Enjoy the experience. You may learn something important about yourself, your colleagues, your chosen profession—even life in general!

Dilemma No. 1

Is Honesty a Personal Quality—Like Shyness?

When I was department administrator of the justice department of the college where I work, two Police Education students were brought to my office by a faculty member. They had been caught cheating on an examination.

I asked them both if they had, in fact, cheated. A flood of excuses followed, accompanied by interesting you-go-first glances from one to the other. It was only after the cheat sheet was produced and clearly matched one of their answers that they grudgingly admitted to cheating.

Then something interesting happened. One of the students became quite emotional, admitted his guilt, said he was ashamed of himself, and said he had learned a painful lesson from the experience.

The other student, on the other hand, continued to be defiant, insisting that many students cheated on examinations. I asked him if he thought that honesty was an important personal quality for a police officer, and he replied, "Well, it would be different if I had a uniform on." There is a curious logic to this response.

Both students were asked about their career aspirations. The defiant student said he wished to join the Ontario Provincial Police force, and the other student said he wanted to join the Royal Canadian Mounted Police force.

Questions

1. Is being honest a personal quality or characteristic—like shyness, for example— or is it something we simply decide to be, depending on the circumstances in which we find ourselves?

2. Is there any moral difference between cheating on an examination, and stealing from an unlocked electronics store while on night patrol as a police officer?

3. If you were me, and you heard six months later that the defiant student was in the final stages of the recruitment process for the Ontario Provincial Police, would you, or should you, pick up the phone and give the recruitment section the information you have?

4. If your answer is no, why not? If yes, why?

5. Is a college professor or administrator's primary responsibility to his graduate student, or to the general welfare of the community?

6. If a person appears subsequently to be genuinely remorseful for a wrongdoing, should this be a mitigating factor in the way the situation is dealt with?

7. Imagine a situation at a police or corrections training centre where in, say, the tenth week of a twelve-week orientation course a student is found cheating on an examination. Would this circumstance warrant, in your view, dismissing that trainee officer from the force?

8. Which of the tools, if any, may help you with this dilemma?

Dilemma No. 2

Thank God for Sick Days

(*Note*: This is a dilemma that can be applied across the board in the justice field. Please be aware that this scenario has the potential to put you on the defensive. Please try to look at the situation as calmly, logically and reasonably as you can.)

South Side Detention Centre is a maximum security institution housing inmates on remand or serving sentences of 90 days or less. It is a government facility, so the staff are public servants.

Recently there have been several reports in the newspapers about the troubling levels of sick leave used by public servants. The average number of sick days (or "sickies" as they say in Australia!) taken during the last year by government workers has been reported and confirmed to be an average of 11 for each employee. In correctional institutions and police forces the average number is 15 per employee. The cost to the taxpayer is estimated to be tens of millions of dollars each year because of the overtime or casual staff needed to provide shift coverage.

The attitude of many of the staff at South Side Detention Centre is that the sick days are one of their benefits. They feel that sick days are provided for in the contract and are there to be used up, whether they are sick or not. "If you don't use them, you lose them," appears to be the prevailing attitude.

You are an officer at the detention centre, and one day you are sitting in the lunch room and you hear the following conversation.

Officer 1: I owe this place nothing. I make no bones about it, if I want to use one of my sick days for a day off I use it, that's all there is about that!

Officer 2: I know I haven't been here long, I don't know too much about what goes on here. My understanding was that those sick days are there for us in case we really are sick.

Officer 1: That's the way most of us felt at one time, but not anymore. If I want a day out with my wife, or a day out fishing, I'm out of here on a sick day.

Officer 2: I'm not sure I would be able to relax. I think I would feel guilty all day long, so I may as well go to work. Besides, what if you get caught?

Officer 1: So what? The boss does it too. We all do it. It's a right. It's in the contract.

Officer 2: I don't mean to sound self-righteous or anything, but isn't it a form of stealing? If I phone in sick when I am not sick, if I go fishing on a sick day, I am being paid to go fishing, aren't I? I am not sure about that.

Officer 1: It can't be wrong because everybody does it.

Questions

1. Is this problem primarily an economic one, or an ethical one?

2. Is it morally defensible to go fishing on a sick day when I am not sick, but when that activity will probably enhance my mental health?

3. Does a manager or senior officer have any more of a responsibility to act morally than a frontline officer has?

4. Is Officer 2 in the dialogue responsible only for her conduct? If she becomes aware of an abuse of the sick leave policy by a colleague, is she morally "on the hook" to do something with that knowledge?

5. Some people say that silence implies consent. What do you think?

6. Let's assume for the sake of argument that a sick day is worth $200. If I take a sick day when I am not sick, isn't this something like taking $200 out of petty cash? If not, why not?

7. Which of the tools, if any, may help you with this dilemma?

8. To what extent, if any, do you think your response to this kind of dilemma would be governed by officer subcultural constraints?

Dilemma No. 3

The Timing Stinks!

The Mount Henry Police Force (the name is fictitious) is a small, municipal force in a semi-rural community in Canada. The force has a chief, deputy chief, five sergeants, and 37 sworn officers. Generally, the force is considered to be well run, and enjoys the respect of the community it serves. The chief is considered to be a politically active individual, and is on good terms—is friends, even—with almost all of the local officials.

It is a damp, cold November evening and Constable James has parked his car in a rest area a few kilometres from the station to get caught up with his paperwork. (James is a probationary constable, with just three months of his 12-month probation remaining.) The roads are quiet and he is enjoying a few moments of peace to collect his thoughts, and to reflect on what has been a long shift.

At that moment the police car in which he sits is illuminated by the headlights of an oncoming car. The headlights are on full and dazzle James for a moment. The car passes him slowly, and when he turns around to take a better look at it, he notices it is being driven erratically. "Thank God," he thinks to himself, "there are no other cars around."

He starts the cruiser, turns on his lights, and swings around in pursuit of the car. As he approaches the car, he notices it is increasing in speed. It veers alarmingly from side to side, and the young officer becomes increasingly anxious at the thought of what might happen if another car happens to approach from the opposite direction.

He makes a quick decision that this is simply too great a risk to take. He accelerates, catches up with the now speeding, veering car, and manages to overtake it. Getting ahead of it, gradually he is able to slow the driver down and get him to come to a stop.

Shaken, and feeling quite angry, he gets out of his cruiser, approaches the vehicle—and shines his torch into the face of the chief of police. The chief explains that he had been to a difficult budget meeting, and afterwards knocked back a few drinks. He had assured his friends, who expressed concern for his safety before he left, that he was fit to drive, especially since it was not far to his home, and along a quiet road.

"Constable James, you're a good man. My house is just up the road; I'll be fine. Good work. I'll remember you for understanding the situation. Those buggers at City Hall don't understand what these budget cuts are going to mean to us. Anyway, whatever happens, even though you are the youngest officer on the force, you have my word that you will not be affected…if you see what I mean."

Questions

1. What should Constable James do?

2. What would you do if you were in a similar situation?

3. Constable James has to think about his wife, his baby, a mortgage and a career he loves. Should his decision be influenced by these responsibilities and concerns? Where should one's priorities lie in situations like this one?

4. Keep in mind your responses to questions 1, 2 and 3. What if you were a police officer pulled over for drunk driving, and the investigating officer, a colleague and friend of yours, chastised you for being a stupid #$°!, but said he was going to give you a break. Should you—would you—accept his kind offer?

5. Should the law be applied in one way for the police "brotherhood" and in another way for ordinary citizens?

6. Which of the tools, if any, may help you with this dilemma?

7. To what extent, if any, do you think your response to this kind of dilemma would be governed by officer subcultural constraints?

Dilemma No. 4

Only Thick-skinned Women Need Apply

The detachment for which you work is in a medium-sized city, and part of a national police force. You are a male officer and you have worked for that police force for the last three years. Generally you enjoy your job, particularly the friendship and camaraderie of your colleagues.

There are 13 officers in the detachment, one of whom is a 23-year-old woman in her first year of work as a police officer. You think she is a dedicated and competent officer, and you also feel that there is a place for such individuals in policing.

She sees you as a decent person with good values, and she also sees you as supportive of her. She comes to you one day, when you are both away from the detachment, and asks you if she can speak with you in confidence. She is looking upset and worried.

She tells you that in the last six months she has

- been told by one sergeant that she would not be a real woman until she had a child, and that she should go home and start a family, preferably with him as the father;

- been grabbed and kissed by a male colleague officer who told her to call him when her husband was away if she wanted a "real man";

- been subjected to viewing a pornographic movie on a night shift in a joint work area; when she complained, her colleagues told her to "hit the road";

- found a pair of plastic breasts taped to her work station with "Police Girl" written on them;

- complained to a supervisor she thought she could count on for support, who advised her to "lighten up."

What she has just told you comes as no surprise to you because these "events" have been common knowledge at the detachment. In fact, when the male officers have been together you have joined them in having a good laugh about the situation.

She trusts you, feels an acute sense of injustice and embarrassment about what she has been subjected to, and wishes to pursue the matter by laying formal harassment complaints against the five officers involved. While you have some significant misgivings about the way she has been treated, you see these five colleagues as good officers, and you enjoy their comradeship. She asks you for your help and support. She wants you to corroborate, as far as you can, her account of the events. But more than anything, she wishes you to help her through what is going to be an extremely difficult ordeal for her.

Questions

1. Should you, and would you, lend the support that is being requested of you?
2. Did you smile when reading this scenario?
3. We have all been subjected to and embarrassed by workplace humour. I remember being sent to a store when I was young to buy a left-handed screwdriver! And one of my former students, all 300 pounds of him, during his first week as a correctional officer, was told to supervise a young offender in the sick room. The shift supervisor told him the young offender was highly dangerous (he wasn't) and that the student was to wear a hockey helmet (several sizes too small) all the time he was supervising the offender. The joke terminated when one of his colleagues took a telltale photograph, recording the event for posterity.

   Are the experiences of the female officer in the dilemma something like the situations I have just described? Or is there something different about them?
4. What are your views about women working in (formerly?) nontraditional occupations, particularly as police or correctional officers?
5. Which of the tools, if any, may help you with this dilemma?
6. To what extent, if any, do you think your response to this kind of dilemma would be governed by officer subcultural constraints?

[*Note*: "Female RCMP officers sexually harassed at work. Six out of 10 surveyed were affected, internal study says." (*The Globe and Mail*, September 27, 1996)]

Dilemma No. 5
I Guess He Should Have Stayed Home

Ted Egan has worked at White Plains Correctional Centre for 13 years. He is a dedicated, competent employee. He is well respected by his colleagues and by the administrators of the institution.

Several times during the last 10 years Egan has been approached by senior officials to encourage him to apply for promotions as they became available in the institution. Each time he declined, explaining he was happy doing what he was doing because it meant he could spend more time with the inmates.

But lately things have not been going very well for Egan. His wife of 21 years has just announced she is filing for divorce. She has met another man. In addition, Egan's 13-year-old daughter is acting rebelliously. Egan, particularly because of the business he is in, is keenly aware of a serious breakdown in communication between himself and his daughter. The marital problems are certainly not making matters any easier.

Now Egan is at work. It has been a difficult shift on this particular day. He reported for work at 7.00 a.m., after an emotionally draining evening and night dealing with problems at home. Clearly, he arrived at work tired and worried. As is often the case at stressful times like this, the inmates seem to sense he isn't his normal self, and start to act out.

One particular inmate is getting on Egan's nerves. He is 18 years old, small and "yappy." He never stops. For several hours he has been carrying on with his high-pitched, pointless, and increasingly maddening "yap."

Egan somehow manages to remain in control of himself; that is, until this particular individual comes into the unit office to complain about some of the other inmates. They had told him in no uncertain terms to "belt up or else." At this moment Egan loses control and slaps the inmate hard across the face. The blow is hard enough to leave a red welt and a small cut. The noise of the blow is loud enough to be heard by the other inmates—who spontaneously break into a round of applause! In 13 years this is the first time that Egan has lost his temper in this way.

Another officer is called to cover Egan's post, and he goes to report the matter to the superintendent. She invites Egan in, and listens intently to someone she normally admires and respects as he recounts the incident.

"I did it," he said. "I hit him hard. He just got to me. Things have not been good at home lately—but that's no excuse. I know you have to fire me. Or would you let me resign? I'm truly sorry it had to happen this way."

Questions

1. If you were the superintendent what should you do? Should you fire Egan? Should you allow him to resign? Should you perhaps take a course of action that is quite different from these two?

2. Should an officer, in a position of public trust, be fired for making one uncharacteristic mistake when there appear to be extenuating circumstances contributing to that mistake?

3. Should the superintendent, in making her decision, take into account the probable effect of Egan's dismissal on the morale of his colleagues? Or is this simply not an issue?

4. Assume that the superintendent made a decision not to fire Egan; let's say in this instance he would be warned and reprimanded. Might the superintendent be in danger of signaling that it is okay to engage in unprofessional conduct, so long as it occurs only infrequently?

5. Should Egan's personal circumstances, and his subsequent attitude of contrition, be a factor in the superintendent's decision?

6. Which of the tools, if any, may help you with this dilemma?

7. To what extent, if any, do you think your response to this kind of dilemma would be governed by officer subcultural constraints?

Dilemma No. 6

A Little Bit of Intimidation

You are a correctional officer at Cedarvale Correctional Centre for Youth. The centre accommodates young offenders on remand. Their ages range from 15 to 18.

You are working the afternoon shift from 3.00 p.m.-11.00 p.m. and, to put it diplomatically, the shift has been "lively." In fact, to put it less diplomatically, it has been the shift from hell! You and your partner are both beginning to fray around the edges. At one point you hear your partner shout at one of the kids, "I have one nerve left and you are getting on it."

One inmate in particular has been getting under the skin of your partner. He is a bullying, loud, unkempt and obnoxious individual. According to the morning shift log, he has been testing the limits all day, and he is still at it.

Your partner suddenly decides that he has had enough. He tells this particular young offender to come to the office, and asks you to come as a witness.

No sooner have the three of you entered the office, than the inmate starts mouthing off again. It seems there is simply no stopping him. He knows no fear. He certainly is not intimidated. "I can't wait to get out of this fucking dump. I'm sick of the fucking slop you give us to eat 'round here. I'm sick of your silly-assed rules," he exclaims. "Fuck the lot of you!"

By this time your partner is getting red in the face, and is clearly close to losing control.

"Now look here, you puke-faced little prick," your partner responds. "You've been in my face all shift long, and I've had it with your fucking attitude. Frankly, you make me sick, and if I were free to punch your fucking lights out, believe me I would. You're smart enough to know we can't do that anymore, you punks have more rights than we have as staff. Anyway, let me tell you something. Since you are going to get out of here, and since you're heading right back to the street and all of your dangerous fucking games, I have no doubt you're going to get right back into the same shit you were in before."

By this time your partner is on a roll! It appears there is no stopping *him*. He is in full flight all right. He continues, "But let me tell you one thing, you little shit-face, I can't wait for the day when you get to the big house. That'll wipe the smile off your face—the first time they rape you, they like fresh-faced boys like you. It'll look good on you. Now get out of my face, and remember this conversation the first time they stick one up you."

Questions

1. This inmate complained to the administration about the manner and content of your partner's "chat" with him. You are asked to write a report about the incident. What do you think you would write?

2. Is it ethical to use fear as a supervisory technique?

3. Do you think you would use a similar technique under similar circumstances?

4. Let's assume that your partner's chat did the trick—that the inmate quieted right down, and as a result became much more manageable for all the officers. Let's also assume that you feel your partner's technique is a dubious one. If the end result is a good one, does that always justify the means by which you achieve it?

5. If an officer uses a fear-inducing technique, is her motive for using that technique important or relevant in deciding whether such a tactic is ethical?

6. You may have heard of a program called Scared Straight in which convicted felons, usually serving life sentences, try to scare young offenders out of a life of crime. Are programs such as these ethical in the way they try to scare young offenders?

7. Which of the tools, if any, may help you with this dilemma?

8. To what extent, if any, do you think your response to this dilemma would be governed by officer subcultural constraints?

Dilemma No. 7

Sleeping Arrangements

You are a relatively new correctional officer at Beach Head Institution. You have worked at the institution for nine months, so there are three months remaining of your one-year probationary period. At that time, with satisfactory reports from supervisors and colleagues, you will become a classified officer—a status that gives you much more security and permanency than if you were an unclassified officer.

Beach Head Institution is a maximum security facility housing male offenders, most of them in jail for having committed violent offences.

You are working a string of seven night shifts that run from 11.00 p.m. until 7.00 a.m. This is the sixth of the seven shifts and you are feeling exhausted. You are not finding it easy to sleep in the daytime, partly because you are not yet used to it, but mainly because your one-year-old daughter is now quite active and noisy.

On this night you are assigned to work with an officer who has worked at Beach Head for the last 17 years. At 2.00 a.m., he approaches you and tells you that he is going to take the next two hours for a sleep, and that you should go on your rounds without him. At 4.00 a.m., he says, you should wake him up, and then it will be your turn for two hours of rest. You are aware that this is strictly against the standing orders of the institution, and that being caught asleep by a senior officer is grounds for dismissal.

You explain to your partner that you feel uncomfortable with the "arrangement," and you insist, for your own safety and the general safety of the area you are patrolling, that you do the rounds together. Your partner becomes highly agitated, asks you who the fuck you think you are, waves his finger in your face, and tells you that you will do as you are told. After calming down a little, he explains to you that he has an important event to attend the following morning, and that he has been banking on getting some sleep during the shift. He reminds you that you are on probation, and that if you think you can do anything about the conversation you have just had, you may as well forget it, because he would be believed and supported over you.

Questions

1. How do you think you *would* handle a situation like this one?

2. What do you think you *should* do?

3. Is it ever ethical to tell one's supervisor about the poor performance or objectionable behaviour of a fellow officer?

4. Let's assume that during the following day you make further surreptitious enquiries about your predicament with someone you trust. You discover that the lieutenants are also in the habit of taking their turns to sleep. Now what?

5. To whom are you primarily responsible:
   Your colleague?
   The inmates?
   Your employer?
   Yourself?
   All, some, or none of the above?

6. Some people are of the view that if one officer knows of another officer's serious indiscretion, but chooses to stay silent, both officers share responsibility for the indiscretion. What do you think?

7. Which of the tools, if any, may help you with this dilemma?

8. To what extent, if any, do you think your response to this dilemma would be governed by officer subcultural constraints?

Dilemma No. 8
Arresting Officer or Judge?

This dilemma is to be looked at from the perspective of someone who is not an officer, but may have been the victim of an officer's lack of judgment, if not wrongdoing. I will attempt to relay the situation to you by simply stating what appear to be the facts. I have made every effort not to "launder" the information. And I have made a conscious effort not to attempt to lead your thinking on this issue.

One evening I received a telephone call from a rather distraught young woman (a former student of mine) informing me that the evening before she had been involved in a serious confrontation with her boyfriend.

She had told him, she claimed, that the relationship was over and that she did not wish to see him again. They argued for approximately four hours, and the argument culminated in a scuffle between them. He punched out the windshield of his car, hit her across the face with the back of his hand, and pulled her hair. She attempted to defend herself by scratching back at him. The police were called and he was charged with assault. She was taken to the local hospital and received treatment for a bruised scalp.

The purpose of her phone call to me, in reality, was not so much to give me this information, as to ask me what the process was for getting the charges against her boyfriend withdrawn. We had a discussion about the issue, and we finished the conversation.

A few days later I was sitting in my office when this same young woman, now seemingly even more distraught than she had been a few days earlier, tapped on the door and asked if she could speak with me. She was accompanied by her friend, who seemed to me to be a reasonable, mature and steady kind of individual. Through the tears, the young woman recounted to me how at 2.30 a.m. that morning she had been awakened by two police officers, one of whom was a woman. She was informed of her rights and the charges, asked to get dressed, taken to the police cruiser, and driven to the police station. Her former boyfriend had decided to lay charges of his own against her, and this arrest in the middle of the night was the result.

During the arrest and subsequent journey to the police station, the male police officer accused her of setting up her boyfriend in what he kept referring to as a "fatal attraction" scenario (from the movie *Fatal Attraction*). He made it clear to her that she was the cause of the problem, that her boyfriend was from a good family and had a girlfriend to whom he was committed. (The boyfriend had informed the young woman that this relationship had terminated four months previously.)

These events have been unfolding as I write this chapter. Just a few evenings ago, a few days after my second conversation with the young woman, she telephoned me to thank me for my help. She told me that she had contracted the help of a lawyer, who had had a conversation with the crown attorney, and that the charges had been dropped.

Questions

1. If you were the female colleague of the arresting male police officer, and the facts of the arrest are as I have described them, what, if anything, would you *wish* to say to your colleague? What do you think you *would* say?

2. Is there something inappropriate about an arresting police officer making a personal judgment about the situation, and, in this instance, comparing the details of the situation to those he has seen in a film?

3. If you think there is something inappropriate about this approach, and the matter comes to your attention (you are now the arresting officer's supervisor), what would be your response to the officer's actions?

4. Let's assume that the senior officer who is investigating the complaint from the young woman asks you, the arresting officer's partner, for your account of the events. How do you think you would respond?

5. Is it possible that there is a gender bias at play in the way the arrest unfolded and in some of the things that were said by the arresting officer?

6. Which of the tools, if any, may help you with this dilemma?

7. To what extent, if any, do you think your response to this dilemma would be governed by officer subcultural constraints?

Summary

These are just a few examples of the sorts of dilemmas and problems that can be encountered. My hope is that you will be challenged by them, but that at the same time you enjoy the process of opening your mind to new and interesting angles and perspectives.

I would encourage you to generate your own scenarios, preferably drawn from your own experience, and to air them with fellow students.

In the meantime, here are some more brainteasers that you may like to ponder:

- Who should police the police?
- If a recruit officer is caught cheating on an examination during the last week of his training, should he be dismissed?
- If and when you are told by your coach officer that you should forget everything you were taught at the academy, college or training centre, what do you think you should do with this information?
- Is there a place for a whistle-blowing officer on any police force or in any correctional institution? If yes, under what circumstances? If no, why not?
- How do you think you would respond to a colleague who appears to be racist, or sexist, or is a bully? Are her attitudes or behaviours any business of yours?
- How do you feel about homosexual officers working in the justice field?
- What place is there for officer discretion? Is it possible for officers to use discretion, and still be considered fair?
- Martin Luther King said there are good laws and bad laws; good laws should be upheld, bad laws should be disobeyed. He was advocating the view that at times there can be a place for civil disobedience. How do you respond to this idea?
- Have you ever considered how you would respond if you were assigned a duty as a police officer that conflicted with your personal values? (For example, there was a case on a large metropolitan police force in which a veteran officer was assigned to ensure the safety of a doctor and his abortion clinic; the officer refused the detail on religious grounds, and was dismissed from the force.)

- One veteran police officer once told me that he knew of no police officer who had not, on at least one occasion, perjured himself. How do you respond to this point of view?
- Is there a place for complicity in report writing?
- Would you ever lie to save a fellow police or correctional officer?
- When you are being questioned about an incident to which you were a party, is the act of omitting important details that are known to you the same as lying? Or not?
- Should police forces and correctional institutions be open to public scrutiny? When asked by one researcher for access to his officers, one police chief responded, "The (name deleted) force has not enjoyed a particularly productive experience with sociological studies of various kinds." Should there be a place for independent, unbiased inquiry into the role of policing and corrections in our society?

9

Reputable Officers

You see, what's happened is that now I've learned this new material [in the ethics course] I've become more accountable. It's pretty frightening when you pay $112 [course fee] and become more accountable. Generally you get paid for being accountable. There is obviously a certain responsibility that comes with an education—this one in particular. — *Journal entry. Justice student in ethics course.*

The Point of the Exercise

I am going to assume that you have courageously had a go at some of the hard questions contained in this book; and that, either on your own or with the gentle or not-so-gentle prodding of your facilitator, you have been as honest as you can be. You may well now be asking the question, What has it all been for? What's the point? Has the exercise been worth it?

In the final analysis, of course, you must answer these questions for yourself, and come to your own conclusions. But in the meantime, let me suggest a few things to you.

First, perhaps it's better to think about the hard questions and tough issues raised in this book in the relative comfort and safety of a classroom, rather than when you are out on the street or on the institution range. I hope there will be some transference value to the thinking and discussing you have been doing during this learning process, so that the difficult decisions you will no doubt have to make on the job will be a little clearer, a little crisper and, perhaps most important, ones with which you will feel comfortable. Even so, the feelings you will be left with after making these decisions, as I have suggested several times, may not be ones of complete peace, because the nature of a dilemma is often that there is no one perfect solution. More often than not, what we would be seeking to make would be the *best* decision rather than the *right* one.

Second, if engaging in this exercise helps just one of you to make a decision that you may not otherwise have made, or helps to prevent you from making one that you may have made and regretted, then I would like to think my work in writing this book—and your effort and diligence in working through it—is justified. I'm thinking here of really important decisions—ones that will define you as a person, and will either contribute to justice, fairness and decency, or detract from these values that we hold in such high esteem.

But whatever your view of these two points, don't relax just yet. We are not quite finished with this process! To conclude the book, there are a few additional points of discussion that I would like to engage you in.

At this point, I am going to express some personal, and perhaps controversial, thoughts on two questions. I express these views simply to encourage you to engage in further dialogue about them, and to leave you with some final ideas to think about. I claim no special wisdom in this regard, and there are no easy answers to these issues. But I am going to take a risk and be a little more forthcoming on these issues than I have been up to this point. I am going to lead with my chin, as it were, and set myself up on a pedestal. Of course, you are quite free to knock me off my perch if you can—so long as you can defend your views. Try to do so, but remember to consider the tools we discussed in Chapter 7. Check to see if they can support your arguments.

Can an Independent Thinker be a Team Player?

One question that you may have been asking yourself—or perhaps the topic has come up in class—is, "If I seek to be my own person as a police officer or correctional officer, how is this going to affect my ability to operate as a team player? Isn't being able to be a team player critical to the role of a police or correctional officer?"

This is a good question, and it is one that needs to be asked. You are correct if you think that this book essentially is about the individual officer, and the ability of that individual to make independent moral decisions and to have the courage to act on those decisions. You are also correct if you think that there may be some implications, in holding this view, for the officer group.

Let me suggest that there is something deeply troubling, and potentially dangerous, about individuals who are prepared to give up their sense of self and their individuality simply to ensure they fit into a particular group. Let me further suggest that if any group expects of any one of us that sort of mindless, unthinking obedience, then surely we should seriously question whether we wish to continue our association with that group.

Now of course I am not suggesting that a correctional officer or police officer group is normally characterised by such an expectation. I am suggesting, however, that there may be moments when we feel that that expectation is very much there. And it is at those moments, as rare as they may be, that how we respond is critically important to our welfare and well-being.

So what are we to do with those odd moments when we feel group pressure bearing down on us to participate in an activity with which we feel considerable discomfort? Is it possible at those moments to be our own person and still continue to be accepted and respected as a team player?

I think it is. And I think so because I have been privileged to meet several officers who have been able to keep that important distinction in their professional lives. The ideas I am going to suggest here, I have learned from them.

First, I think we owe it to each other as members of a colleague group to be up front with each other. When I ask people in my seminars what names they have for officers who break ranks and report a colleague, the word "snitch" is one of the first ones mentioned. "Snitching" is a pejorative word because it implies our running behind a person's back to tell something to someone, normally a person in authority. It implies acting in an underhanded way. Often this can be a destructive, demoralizing behaviour, and I would question its value or propriety in the context of policing or corrections. Something similar can be said, of course, of other professions. But in the context of policing and corrections, where being there for each other is so important, and where trust is critical, it is imperative that we seek ways to let our colleagues know exactly how we are responding personally when something is bothering us. This will require moral courage. It will be risky. But would this approach not be a better option than choosing to be devious and underhanded in the way we address what we consider to be a wrongdoing?

Of course, there may be times when we may be so troubled by something that is happening, and so terribly scared of the possibility of colleague retribution, that the only solution available to us is to go and speak with a senior officer in confidence. That is an option that each of us can consider when we feel we are caught.

How the senior officer responds to your request for anonymity will be interesting for you to discover. If he or she guarantees you anonymity and then you deliver some information about which she simply must do something, this will present a rather obvious dilemma for that officer. There's the commitment made to you by her versus her professional and ethical responsibility to do something with the new piece of information. If the manager feels she cannot guarantee you anonymity, and she tells you this at the outset, then, of course, she runs the risk of not finding out something that is clearly important.

What would you do in this situation if you were the manager? Would you commit to holding the information and the person conveying it in complete confidence, prior to knowing what the information is? Let's continue our discussion.

What we need to aim for, I would suggest, is to establish a climate in a policing or corrections context where we, as officers, give each other permission to approach each other in an open and honest way when something is not sitting well. If you feel this is a kind of pipe dream, something that is completely unrealistic, then we need to ask ourselves the question, Why would it be so unrealistic to expect this kind of agreement between a group of people who have sworn to uphold law and order? What about those situations, you may ask, where we feel that simply discussing the situation with our colleague is not going to be enough. The situation is serious enough that we feel the truth must come out. Well, here I can say to my colleague something like this, "I feel really bad about your putting your uniform on when you're not on shift to get free meals from the Chinese restaurant, and I think it is wrong of you to do that; we're not supposed to take gratuities when we are on shift, let alone do what you are doing. It's up to you, I have spoken with you several times about this, and you have not taken me seriously. Either you come clean about it, or you will leave me no alternative but to report it. You are making all of us look bad. I can't stay quiet about this."

The officer in question, you will have noted, is not only compromising himself and his force by accepting gratuities, but he is also gaining the gratuities by deceitful means. There are two wrongs here.

I told you I was going to lead with my chin, didn't I? Would it be a fair assumption that this suggestion is eliciting a fairly strong emotional response in you? *No*? That's interesting. *Yes*? Why do you think you are reacting as you are?

If you are reacting negatively to what I have suggested, perhaps you can tell me how else we should approach issues of wrongdoing? If I remain silent about my colleague's inappropriate conduct I am, in effect, condoning it. Some folk have suggested that silence implies consent, and that if I know of a wrongdoing and keep quiet about it I am equally guilty.

What obviously gets in the way of justice being served at these moments is my feelings for, and my loyalty to my colleagues, right? These are noble sentiments, and such loyalty and concern for each other in our dangerous workplace is so important. But what if it leads to abuse, corruption, cover-up, injustice, and betrayal of public trust? What then? What about the public you serve and the trust they have placed in you as a peace officer to do the right thing? What about your own commitment to honesty, impartiality, fairness, justice, equity and human rights?

Another important question may be, Is there a possibility that if educators introduce you the student to this ethics experience, and it serves to reinforce your moral sense and contributes to your becoming keener than ever to fulfil your duties in a highly principled way, it might set you up for disappointment and bewilderment once you join the ranks of the officer group?

As I write this book in mid-1997, there has recently been an inquiry into police corruption in New South Wales, Australia. As a result of what can only be described as a scathing indictment of the force by a royal commission, new police recruits in that state now are required in their training to participate in an ethics educational experience.

In May 1997, the first 219 police graduates of the new training program were sworn in as probationary constables. "Class 268 had learnt about ethics and the 'highest possible standards' during their time at the academy, and they 'must never tolerate, never ignore' corruption, the abuse of police powers or poor service delivery," said Peter Ryan, the Police Commissioner. One graduate, in an interview is reported to have said, "Just do the right thing and keep my nose clean—and whatever you see, you have to report it." Another graduate said, "I think those [corrupting] temptations are always there, but what they're trying within the recruiting system now is basically to be able to avoid that temptation, and look at moral strengths among their recruits rather than selecting people that may be swayed." (*The Sydney Morning Herald*, May 17, 1997). Is this idealism, as laudable as it is, inherently risky or even dangerous for the new recruit? The group, as we have suggested, can be set in its ways, and is often characterized by the norm that the officer's commitment to his colleague group should be honoured above all else.

This question about whether we may be setting up recruits for failure is a good one, and there is no easy answer. We clearly do not wish you, as new officers, to leave your educational experience like white knights riding all-knowing chargers, acting as though you have a lock on morality. The officer group has its own ways of dealing with new officers who come on in this way, and the correcting experience can be a painful one!

Let me suggest, however, that any ethics educational experience within the context of a justice program would be incomplete without talking about the officer group and its dynamics, including the subcultural constraints issue. I remember one graduate of a two-year police education program telling me that there had been no mention at all during her studies of what she might have anticipated in terms of colleague group pressures.

Perhaps it is only by fully informing you about the subculture and how it may impact on you—the new officer or would-be officer—that you will be prepared for what you may expect on the job. Then what you do with your moral idealism is up to you. Somehow you will have to look for ways to quietly and humbly convey your personal standards in a way that is not going to get you on the wrong side of your colleagues.

Look around you, see who you admire. Who best exemplifies a sense of true professionalism and decency in the way he does the job? Model yourself on that officer. Tell him of your respect, and seek his advice and help.

Should We Admit to Wrongdoing?

What do you think is the best policy: to admit to a wrongdoing one has committed, or not? I guess for almost every person who chooses not to admit to a wrongdoing and is subsequently found out, there are an equal number of people who benefit from covering up their wrongdoing. I have no statistics to support this view, and I may be wrong, but that's my sense of the way things are.

If I am correct in my assumption, then there would appear, at first blush, to be some advantage in at least attempting to cover up a wrongdoing, right? This would apply especially in cases where it is known that it is going to be difficult for the investigators to produce evidence of the wrongdoing.

Many of us seem to have a natural tendency to deny responsibility when we are confronted about a wrongdoing; perhaps this kind of defensiveness has its roots in our instinct for survival. There are probably few of us who have not engaged in lying in an attempt to save our skins. I am as guilty as anyone else in this regard. Would you agree that these moments when we engage in this kind of defensiveness and deceitfulness are moments that are not easily forgotten?

There are moments in each of our lives that I call defining moments. They are made up of experiences that deeply affect us in one way or another, for good or ill, and that leave us changed in some way.

Let me be quite personal with you at this point as I tell you about one such defining moment in my life. I grew up in rural Wales. I lived in a tiny village called Little Honeyborough. The village consisted of 10 cottages, two farms and a chapel. As a child I was encouraged (no, told!) by my parents to go to the chapel every Sunday. There wasn't much of a protest from my brothers and sisters and me, because when I think about it now, the chapel was the social centre of the village. (I can imagine you muttering as you read this, *Get a life!*)

One big event of the year was the Sunday School fete. It was a fundraising, fun event, with various market stalls and innocent games booths. One year—I think I must have been about 10 years of age at the time—it was my job, along with another Sunday School "scholar," to operate a booth where the idea was to throw table-tennis balls into goldfish bowls, much like you would see at some fairs now. For threepence (a few cents) a go you could have three shots at winning a goldfish!

During the day, my fellow helper excused himself for a bit, and I was left on my own to operate the stall. It was at this point that the defining moment took place. I helped myself to (stole) half a crown (two shillings and sixpence), worth about 50 or 60 cents now, but worth much more then. The fact that the cash tin was short was noticed by my colleague when he returned. He spoke with me first, and then to one of the organizers, about the missing money. I was questioned regarding the missing money, and of course I denied knowing anything about it.

The guilty feelings associated with that incident remain with me to this day, many years later. This was a really defining moment in my life even at that early age, because it forced me to face up to the struggle between right and wrong. It also introduced me, perhaps in a way that hadn't happened to the same extent prior to that experience, to the anguish of deep guilt. In retrospect, I regretted then, and regret now, not admitting to taking the money. I often wonder how this event may have affected me differently had I done so. In any event, there is no doubt in my mind now, that the nonverbal signals I would have been giving off during the discussions about the missing money would have literally screamed that I was the guilty party. So not only would the organizers have known that I had taken the money, but they would have known I was a liar.

It's interesting, but even though I think I learned much from what may appear to others to be a rather innocuous experience, the temptation is still very much there to lie or to be evasive when confronted. It is almost as though the defensive reaction is a primeval one. My wife would no doubt confirm this for you! Am I alone in exaggerating traffic problems when late for dinner? Or in coming up with some ingenious "reason" (and it would have to be ingenious) why an important occasion has been overlooked?

Now let's attempt to relate these meandering thoughts to life as a police or correctional officer.

If I make a mistake—if I screw up, to use the vernacular—should I admit to my wrongdoing? In the final analysis, of course, we have to make our own decisions. No one should or can make them for us.

I pull the trigger too hastily in my panic; I fall asleep on night shift, and due to my neglect an inmate takes the opportunity to hang himself; I allow myself to become tunnel-visioned in a case I am investigating, and because of my investment in the case I refuse to consider new evidence that indicates the accused is the wrong person; I allow myself to be duped into taking a "compassionate" letter out of the institution for an inmate, the contents of which subsequently contribute to drugs being brought into the facility.

During the investigations that will inevitably take place into incidents like these, should I be honest and aboveboard, or should I attempt to get myself out of the tough spot by lying?

This is a difficult question, and one you must address to yourself. Do some thinking about it now, so that you may be better prepared for struggling with it if and when the time comes.

Meanwhile, let me offer you some thoughts on this question about owning responsibility for wrongdoing. Again, these ideas are offered simply in the interests of sparking some of your own thinking and discussion.

Would you agree that we are, generally, much more ready to forgive someone who has made a mistake, and who admits to that mistake, than we are to forgive someone whom we think is clearly guilty and whom we feel is lying and cheating? This is a rather curious response, if I am right in thinking that most of us instinctively, when we have done something wrong, feel a great temptation to get into a defensive mode. Maybe this is the reason we think it is so laudable when some individuals can overcome the natural urge to lie, and be big enough to accept responsibility for their actions.

As human beings, we are all too familiar with our predilection for making mistakes, and with our tendency from time to time to engage in wrongdoing. But even when the wrongdoing is serious, if the person making the mistake is courageous enough to admit to it, we can be forgiving. This is probably because we identify with the person as one imperfect human being to another.

You may remember one of the dilemmas we discussed (Number 5), in which an officer had uncharacteristically hit a young offender and was subsequently contrite about his indiscretion. Didn't you feel for the officer when you were discussing the dilemma? And what about the two students who were brought to me for cheating on an examination (Number 1)? One student, you may remember, was very defensive about the whole affair, and the other was ashamed and embarrassed about what he did. Doesn't a person's subsequent response to his mistake make a difference to the way we respond to him?

I think it would be wise to offer a word of caution here, however. A false act of "contrition," an apology or an accepting of the responsibility for a wrongdoing that is offered without sincerity, is, without putting too fine a point on it, manipulative. As humans, we generally have our antennae out for this kind of manipulative behaviour, and it often makes us much less forgiving of the wrongdoer.

Would you agree that we seem to have a sixth sense about whether someone is truly contrite or not? Of course, there will always be occasions when we can be duped, but normally we seem to know instinctively if a person's response is genuine.

As I write these lines, a week ago there was a heavyweight boxing match between Mike Tyson and Evander Holyfield. Some of you may remember that during the fight Tyson bit both of Holyfield's ears, tearing a small piece out of one of them. The fight was stopped by the referee, who disqualified Tyson. Yesterday at a press conference, Tyson read what appeared to be a carefully scripted statement saying he was sorry for what he had done. But in my view, there was no *heart* in what he said. There was little of him as a human being in his words—probably because the words he read were not his own. It should not be surprising that many folk have since raised an eyebrow over this act of "contrition," and remain unconvinced that Tyson really felt that he did anything wrong.

So would it be fair to say that as humans we do not respond well to people who attempt to lie their way through an investigation of wrongdoing? And that we do not respond well to people who, having been found to have committed a wrongdoing, indulge in what appears to be a fake act of contrition?

As I write this chapter, a female first lieutenant in the U.S. military has just faced a court martial on a charge of having committed adultery while serving as an officer in the military. Lieut. Kelly Flinn, America's first woman B-52 bomber pilot, received what is called a "general discharge" from the military. This book is not the place to debate the U.S. military's policies around officers' sexual conduct, but it is interesting to note that military senior personnel cited Lieut. Flinn's alleged initial dishonesty and denial as one of the mitigating factors in their decision to discharge her from the service. That would seem to imply that had there been a more straightforward, honest initial response from her, the decision might have been a different one.

I can't tell you what you should do at those moments when you find yourself on the hot seat, just as you can't tell me. But perhaps it would be worth keeping in mind how positively we generally respond to people who accept responsibility for their mistakes, and how negatively we generally respond to people who are evasive.

There is one additional factor to think about. We should consider how we would feel about ourselves if we managed to get away with a wrongdoing by lying about it. If we are able to take comfort from, or gloat about, such a hollow victory, perhaps we should think seriously about whether or not we continue to be worthy of the important law-keeping role in society we enjoy or are seeking.

One officer I once spoke with, who had been reprimanded for committing a serious indiscretion about which he had responded honestly, said, "At least I can live with myself; I knew what I did was wrong, but I felt that I had to take responsibility for it." When this person said this, I have to say he went up in my estimation for the mature way in which he accepted ownership of his actions. Although the act committed clearly would meet with our disapproval, would you not agree that this officer's response is one to be admired?

Let's draw to a conclusion these thoughts on whether or not it is wise to admit to wrongdoing. Today as I write these notes, the report of the inquiry commission investigating accusations of wrongdoing by the Canadian military in Somalia (referred to in Chapter 1) was published. Here are some comments made by the commissioners about two of the principal players in that affair. Of Gen. Jean Boyle, the commissioners report: "We are satisfied...that Gen. Boyle was a party to the decision to informally release altered documents...and that he knew of such alterations. We are satisfied...that Gen. Boyle participated in the devising of a process which provided the public with misleading or incomplete information and condoned such a process." But of Maj.-Gen. Lewis Mackenzie, they had this to say: "Gen. Mackenzie is unique among the leaders who appeared before us....[He] testified before us in an honest and straightforward manner. He alone seemed to understand the necessity to acknowledge error and account for his personal shortcomings....His comportment and demeanour throughout his testimony before us were consistent with the highest standards of military duty and responsibility." (*The Globe and Mail*, July 3, 1997, p. A4.)

What is important to note is that the commissioners did not find Maj.-Gen. Mackenzie blameless. He had made serious mistakes. The commission found that, "Maj.-Gen. Mackenzie's fundamental failing was that he exercised inappropriate control and provided inadequate supervision." (*The Globe and Mail*, July 3, 1997, p. A4). He made his mistakes, but what separated him from the other leaders in the minds of the commissioners was his willingness to accept responsibility for those mistakes.

I offer this example as support for the personal opinion I have been expressing: we can be forgiving of the wrongdoings and mistakes of others. This is especially the case if we feel that they are willing and prepared to respond honestly, and to take personal responsibility for their mistakes.

Please do with this discussion what you will. Think about it. Think about how you respond to people you have known who have been big enough to admit a mistake or a wrongdoing. Think about those individuals you have judged to be guilty who continue to deny responsibility. Think about manipulative "contrition."

I would encourage you to incorporate that thinking into your own personal decision-making as you do the important work you do.

A Matter of Public Trust

If you are reading these final paragraphs, you have done some of the hard thinking demanded of you by this text. You are to be commended for accepting the challenge.

Perhaps your experience, like that of many of my students, has been that the process of seeking to answer the questions posed left you with a headache; that there were classes and group discussions that you left with your head spinning. Good! Your brain is a muscle just like your other muscles, and if your head ached it probably means that your brain had a bit of a workout. Or perhaps your headaches were caused by the tension you experienced because your values were challenged. I am pleased you were courageous enough to complete the exercise.

It is my sincere wish that you have benefitted from this process in some small way, and that it has contributed to your development as a human being. It is also my sincere wish that you will do well in your career as an officer—the public you serve is depending on you. You will enjoy—as a relatively new officer or when you are hired—an enormous amount of public trust. Keep that trust sacred, and always seek to make the best decisions you can.

You will have noticed that I used the word *best*. I could have used the word *right*. If you know what the right thing to do is, and you do it, you are to be congratulated. But there will be other issues and dilemmas with which you will be confronted, which will not be quite so clear-cut. Here you will have to do what you can to make the best decision under the circumstances. At these moments those exercises may be of some help to you.

I wish you well. Be a good person. Be a good officer. Always do what you consider to be the right thing, or the best thing under the circumstances, as the case may be. Uphold the law, and what you consider to be the truth; seek to carefully and honestly consider where the truth lies. Be consistent. Be fair. Beware of colleagues who may seem to have lost their moral sense, and who aim to drag you down with them.

Above all, in whatever you do and wherever you go, seek at all times to be your own person. Work out for yourself the place that colleague loyalty shall have in the way you do your job, and what the limits of that loyalty are for you.

We have two black-and-tan basset hounds at home. We adopted them in a moment of weakness and have loved them ever since! Suzie is the brains of the outfit, and Sam is as thick as two short planks. But both are lovable. One of the selling features brought to our attention by the previous owner was that Sam "sings." One mention of that word and he develops a funny look on his face, contracts his stomach and, 10 or 20 seconds later, emits a sound that would be enough to make even the most devout person doubt the existence of God. The interesting thing is that when Sam starts to "sing," Suzie starts to bark. The noise can be deafening. Our neighbours also have two dogs, and when ours bark, theirs bark. And if there were other dogs in the neighbourhood, I have no doubt they would be at it, too. Why am I telling you all this?

Here's one last thought for you to take with you. Think about it, and work out for yourself what the message may be for us as human beings. There is an old Chinese proverb that goes something like this: One dog barks, and a hundred others bark at the sound.

As human beings, and as officers, are we that much different from our canine friends?

You be the judge.

References

Baker, Mark (1985). *Cops*. Simon and Schuster Inc., New York.

Baron, Jonathan (1990). "Thinking About Consequences." *Journal of Moral Education*, Vol. 19, No. 2, 77–87.

Beck, Clive (1991). "Approaches to Values Education." *Course Material: Learning Values in Adulthood*, Ontario Institute for Studies in Education, Toronto.

Beck, Clive (1991). "How Adults Learn Values." *Course Material: Learning Values in Adulthood*, Ontario Institute for Studies in Education, Toronto.

Beck, Clive (1991). "Moral Values." *Course Material: Learning Values in Adulthood*, Ontario Institute for Studies in Education, Toronto.

Bittner, E. (1980). *The Function of Police in Modern Society*. Oelegeschalger, Gunn, and Haire, Cambridge, Massachusetts.

Bok, Derek (1988). "Can Higher Education Foster Higher Morals?" *Business and Society Review*, Volume 66, 4–12.

Buscaglia, Leo (1978). *Love*. Fawcett-Crest, New York.

Callaghan, Daniel and Sissela Bok, eds. (1980). *Ethics Teaching in Higher Education*. Hastings Centre on Ethics, Plenum Press, New York and London.

Cartwright, Darwin and Alvin Zander, eds. (1968). *Group Dynamics: Research and Theory*. Harper and Row, Publishers.

Chidley, Joe (1995, January 30). "Bonding and Brutality." *Maclean's*, p. 30.

Coffey, Alan, Edward Eldefonso and Walter Hartinger (1982). *Human Relations: Law Enforcement in a Changing Community* (Third Edition). Prentice Hall, New Jersey.

Collins English Dictionary (Third Editon). 1991. Harper Collins Publishers, London.

Davis, Michael (1990). "Who Can Teach Workplace Ethics?" *Teaching Philosophy*, 21–38.

Desroches, Frederick J. (1986). "The Occupational Subculture of the Police." In: Brian K. Cryderman and Chris N. O'Toole, eds. *Police, Race and Ethnicity: A Guide for Law Enforcement Officers*. Butterworths, Toronto, 39–51.

Dimanno, Rosie (1995, January 30). Attacks on Kerr a punishment for breaking ranks. *The Toronto Star*, p. A6.

Folse, Kimberly A. (1991). "Ethics and the Profession: Graduate Student Training." *Teaching Sociology*, Vol. 19, 344–350.

Fox, Vernon (1983). *Correctional Institutions*. Prentice Hall, New Jersey.

Goldstein, H. (1990). *Problem-oriented Policing*. McGraw-Hill, New York.

Grossi, Elizabeth L. and Bruce L. Berg (1991). "Stress and Job Dissatisfaction Among Correctional Officers: An Unexpected Finding." *International Journal of Offender Therapy and Comparative Criminology*, 35(1), 79.

Hess, Henry (1996, October 23). Former constable describes tampering. *The Globe and Mail*, p. A9.

Horin, Adele. (1994, July 9). Why loyalty is a two-way street. *The Sydney Morning Herald*.

Janis, Irving L. (1968). "Group Dynamics Under Conditions of External Danger." In: *Group Dynamics—Research and Theory*. Darwin Cartwright and Alvin Zander, eds. Harper and Row, Publishers.

Josephson, Michael. "The Bell, the Book, the Candle." The Josephson Institute for Ethics, California.

Kauffman, Kelsey (1988). *Prison Officers and their World*. Harvard University Press, Cambridge, Massachusetts.

Klofas, John and Hans Toch (1982). "The Guard Subculture Myth." *Journal of Research in Crime and Delinquency*, July, 238–254.

Kohlberg, Lawrence (1984). *Essays on Moral Development, Vol. II: The Psychology of Moral Development*. Harper and Row, San Francisco.

Lamont, Leonie. Force's hope for the future seeks a keen eye and a clean nose (1997, May 17). *The Sydney Morning Herald*, 8.

Levy, Harold (1997, March 7). Courtroom 'tense' for detective in shooting. *The Toronto Star*, p. A6.

Lickona, Thomas (1976). "What Does Moral Psychology Have to Say?" In: *Moral Development and Behaviour: Theory, Research and Social Issues*. Lickona, Thomas, Gilbert Geis and Lawrence Kohlberg, eds. Holt, Rinehart, Winston, New York.

Main, Eron. Discretion no part of valour. (1996, October 1). *The Globe and Mail*, p. A16.

Martinson, Barbara, ed. (1987). *A Discourse on Ethics and the Corporate Workplace: Can Ethics be Taught?* Working Paper No. 2. Corporate Council on the Liberal Arts, Working Paper Series, New York.

Mascoll, Philip (1996, November 21). Disciplinary muscle proposed for chief. *The Toronto Star*, p. A6.

Millar, Cal and Philip Mascoll (1995, March 17). Four officers suspended in probe. *The Toronto Star*, p. A6.

Mills, Theodore (1967). *The Sociology of Small Groups*. Prentice Hall, Englewood, N.J.

Noddings, Nel (1994). "Conversation as Moral Education." *Journal of Moral Education*, Vol. 23, No. 2, 107–118.

Paul, Richard (1992). *Critical Thinking*. (Revised Second Edition). Foundation for Critical Thinking, Sonoma State University, Rohnert Park, California.

Sheehy, G. (1977). *Passages: Predictable Crises in Adult Life*. Bantam, New York.

Strike, Kenneth A., Emile J. Haller, and Jonas F. Soltis (1988). *The Ethics of School Administration*. Teachers College Press, New York.

Tafoya, William (1995). "Ethics and the Realities of Life: Surviving the Vortex." In: *Morality in Criminal Justice*. Daryl Close and Nicholas Meier, eds. Wadsworth Publishing Company.

Task Force on Ethics (1985). The University of Alberta. Alberta University, Edmonton. The Senate.

Task Force on Ethics (1988). Progress Review: The University of Alberta. Alberta University, Edmonton. The Senate.

Weber, Max (1967). In: *Essays in Sociology*. Gerth, H.H. and C. Wright Mills, eds. New York and Oxford University Press.

Index

A

Accountability, 9
Advice-giving, 22
Anti-administration, 71
Anti-criminal, 69-70
Anti-public, 71
Australia, 12
New South Wales, 104, 140
Authoritarianism, 37
Autonomy, 85

B

Baker, Mark, 66, 69, 70, 77
Baron, Jonathon, 38, 39
Beck, Clive, 22, 23, 37, 84, 85
Bell, the 102, 110
Benefit maximization, 99, 101, 110
Berg, Bruce, 7, 8, 9, 44, 45, 48, 84
Bernhardt, Michael, 86, 87
Biases, 6
Bittner, E., 45
Blue wall of silence, 87. *See also*
Police, brotherhood
Bok, Derek, 5
Bok, Sissela, 21, 24, 38
Book, the, 103, 110
Boyle, Jean, 145
Buscaglia, Leo, 34

C

Callaghan, Daniel, 21, 24, 38
Canada, 8, 12
Canadian Airborne Regiment, 9
Canadian troops, 8, 9
Candle, the, 103, 110
*Caring: A Feminine Approach
to Ethics and Moral
Education*, 23
Cartwright, Darwin, 45
Caruso, Richard, 51
Chandler, John, 17
Coffey, Alan, 45
Collins English Dictionary , 43
Conduct
code of, 48, 65
informal code of, 44
inmate code of, 65
unwritten rules of, 23, 61
*Cops: Their Lives in Their Own
Words*, 66, 69, 70, 77
Corcoran State Penitentiary,
California, 51, 52
Correctional Institutions, 50, 65, 72
Courage, 12, 106, 137
moral, 6, 85, 115, 138
Critical thinking, 31, 105, 110
five elements of, 106
four characteristics of, 39

D

Dangerous bonding, 9
Davis, Michael, 22
Decision-making
    moral, 9, 19, 63, 105, 137
    seven tools for, 97-109
De-individuation, 9, 54, 65
Desroches, Frederick, 7, 8, 9, 44
Dilemmas, 12
    moral, 99-100
Discourse on Ethics, 17
Dobbing in a mate, 53
Dreilinger, Craig, 23

E

Education
    conditioning, 33-34, 35
    learning climate, 31, 33
    police and corrections training
        academies, 34
    teacher-centered, 34
    value shift, 61
Eldefonso, Edward, 45
Equal respect, 101-102, 110
Ethics
    awareness, 23
    'booster shots', 22
    education, 21
    education in justice training,
        19, 140
    expert, 17
    role of the educator, 28-29, 33, 38
    seminars, 22
    'teaching ethics', 16, 20, 36
        collaborative approach, 23
        prescriptive approach, 23, 83, 84
        prudence approach, 22
    university survey of, 20

Ethics School of Administration,
    The, 99
*Ethics Teaching in Higher
    Education*, 24
Ethos, 9. *See also* Subculture
Excessive force, 82

F

Fink, 53
Flinn, Kelly, 144
Folse, Kimberly, 32
Fox, Vernon, 50, 65, 72

G

Globe and Mail, The, 10, 145
Goldstein, H., 45
Grossi, Elizabeth, 7, 8, 9, 44, 45,
    48, 84
Gzowski, Peter, 9

H

Haller, Emil, 99
Hand-up cop, 88, 95
Hartinger, Walter, 45
Harvard University, 5
Hitler, Adolf, 39
Holyfield, Evander, 144
Horin, Adele, 87

I

Imaginary video camera, 103, 110
Indoctrination, 28-29, 30, 31
    lurking dangers of, 19, 36, 38
    perception of, 36
Inmate hierarchy, 68
Integrity, 89

J

Janis, Irving, 50
Josephson Ethics Institute, The, 102
Josephson, Michael, 102

K

Kauffman, Kelsey, 48, 49
King, Martin Luther, 132
King, Rodney, 103
Klofas, John, 69
Kohlberg, Lawrence, 86, 108-109, 111

L

Loyalty, 60, 84, 87, 95
    to colleagues, 9, 11, 96, 139
    code of, 10
    norm of, 53, 66
Lickona, Thomas, 86

M

Mackenzie, Lewis, 145
Maclean's, 9
Main, Eron, 10, 11
Martinson, Barbara, 17
Massachusetts prison system, 48
Maturity, 12
Metropolitan Toronto Police, 66, 71
Mills, Theodore, 45
Morality, 17, 84, 96
    "means-end", 96
Morals, 7
    stages of development,
        108-109, 111
Moral behaviour, 21
Moral thinking, 38, 42
Morningside, 9

N

Musk-ox syndrome, 71-72
My Lai massacre, 86

Narc, 53
Noddings, Nel, 23
Non-progressive officers, 69
Norms, 7, 18, 59
    officer-related, 48, 49
    group, 69
North, Oliver, 39

O

Ogloff, James, 9

P

Passages: Predictable Crises in Adult Life, 85
Paul, Richard, 36
Peer pressure, 9. *See also* Subcultural constraints
Peer support, 8
Pluralistic ignorance, 69
Police
    brotherhood, 47
    officer solidarity, 49
Prejudices, 6
Principled moral thought, 86
Principles
    benefit maximization, 99, 101
    ethical, 99-102
    equal respect, 101
Prinsloo, Maureen, 67
Prison Officers and their World, 48
Progressive officers, 69
Protective custody, 53
Put on the grease, 51, 61

R

Rat, 51, 52, 53, 61, 62, 77
Ratting out, 51, 61, 67
Responsibility, 9, 141, 143
   moral, 90
Rice, Dan, 23
Role-reversal, 107-108
Royal Military College of Canada, 10
Ryan, Peter, 140

S

Self-esteem, 83
Self-respect, 95
Setting limits, 97
Setting-related stressors, 48
Sheehy, Gail, 85
60 Minutes, 51, 104
Snitch, 138
Socrates, 17
Solid, 65, 68
Solidarity, 49, 60, 66, 76, 84
   group, 50, 96
Soltis, Jonas, 99
Somalia, 9, 145
Somali Inquiry, 9, 10, 86
Special Handling Unit, 51
Stand-up cop, 88, 95
Subculture, 7, 9, 18, 43-46, 50, 54,
   58-73
   correctional officers and, 42, 45,
     46, 48, 50, 65
   'enemies' and, 69
   inmates and, 47, 53, 65, 68
   military and, 9
   officer and criminal links in, 64-68
   police and, 42, 45, 46, 50, 71

positive qualities in, 53
   workplace and, 50
Subcultural constraints, 9, 18, 21, 42,
   43, 63, 86
   gender differences in, 63
Subcultural norms, 48-49, 76-77
Super protective custody, 53
Sydney Morning Herald, The, 87

T

Tafoya, William, 87, 88, 89, 95, 114
Tate, Preston, 51
Thinking about consequences, 38
Toch, Hans, 69
Toronto Star, The, 9, 49, 54, 67, 71
Tyson, Mike, 144

U

Unethical practices, 67, 88
University of Alberta Task Force on
   Ethics, 19
University of Alberta Task Force on
   Ethics: Progress Review, 19
University of Toronto, 22
Unofficial military code, 10
Us versus them, 69, 70

V

Values, 20, 44, 45
   group, 8, 45
   inheriting, 7
   learned, 17
   system, 84
   testing, 7
Vortex, 87

W

Wallace, Mike, 52
Webb, G. L., 45
Weber, Max, 38
Wisdom, 17

Y

Z